VEGAN BOWL ATTACK!

"I've admired Jackie Sobon's cooking and photography skills since the day I laid eyes on her recipes. She understands what it takes to make quality food in your own kitchen and executes that wonderfully in this book."

—**Mary Mattern**, author of *Nom Yourself: Simple Vegan Cooking*

"Jackie's blog was one of the first resources I found that helped me learn how to cook vegan and enjoy it. Her recipes are consistently drool-worthy, creative, fun, and, most importantly, delicious."

—**Emily von Euw**, author of *The Rawsome Vegan Cookbook*

"*Vegan Bowl Attack!* is a must-have addition to your kitchen library. Jackie takes the simplicity of bowl food and elevates it to ninja level. The originality of these approachable recipes will appeal to all skill levels. Looking for that quick meal and simple bowl of health or just want to impress your foodie friends and family with your badass kitchen skills? This book has you covered!"

—**Chad Sarno**, chef, author, and vice president of culinary wellness at Rouxbe Cooking School

VEGAN BOWL ATTACK!

More Than 100
One-Dish Meals
Packed with
Plant-Based Power

JACKIE SOBON

FAIR WINDS

Brimming with creative inspiration, how-to projects, and useful information to enrich your everyday life, Quarto Knows is a favorite destination for those pursuing their interests and passions. Visit our site and dig deeper with our books into your area of interest: Quarto Creates, Quarto Cooks, Quarto Homes, Quarto Lives, Quarto Drives, Quarto Explores, Quarto Gifts, or Quarto Kids.

First published in 2016 by Fair Winds Press,
an imprint of The Quarto Group,
100 Cummings Center, Suite 265-D,
Beverly, MA 01915, USA.
T (978) 282-9590 F (978) 283-2742
www.QuartoKnows.com

Fair Winds Pres titles are also available at discount for retail, wholesale, promotional, and bulk purchase. For details, contact the Special Sales Manager by email at specialsales@quarto.com or by mail at The Quarto Group, Attn: Special Sales Manager, 401 Second Avenue North, Suite 310, Minneapolis, MN 55401, USA.

20 19 18 17   6 7 8 9 10

ISBN: 978-1-59233-721-7

Digital edition published in 2016
eISBN: 978-1-63159-166-2
Library of Congress Cataloging-in-Publication Data available.

Design: Sarkar Design Studio
Page Layout: Megan Jones Design
Photography and cover image: Jackie Sobon

Printed in China

The information in this book is for educational purposes only. It is not intended to replace the advice of a physician or medical practitioner. Please see your health-care provider before beginning any new health program.

THIS BOOK IS DEDICATED TO ALL OF
THE PEOPLE WHO BELIEVE IN ME;
YOU GIVE ME THE STRENGTH TO
FOLLOW MY PASSIONS AND DREAMS.

Contents

INTRODUCTION

Welcome to my not-so-little book of bowls! I am Jackie Sobon, recipe developer, food photographer, and creator of the popular vegan food blog *Vegan Yack Attack*. My focus is always on creating awesome recipes using plant-based, natural ingredients in a fun, easy, and most importantly—delicious—way. A wonderful way to combine all of these aspects into one package is by creating one-bowl meals, and that is what this book is all about.

I've spent roughly 80 percent of the past few years thinking about food. That may sound like an exaggeration, but I'm not kidding when I say that food is something that I love every aspect of. My background is in product design, so aesthetics are very important to me; but one dynamic that I was taught about in school was the principle of "form follows function." That being said, I believe that when it comes to food, form is just as important as function. Food tastes better when it looks better!

This cookbook embodies its title wholeheartedly in that it offers fun, delicious, and creative food in bowls (the best vessel of all, in my opinion). From unique recipes to revamped traditional dishes that make you nostalgic and lots of healthy meals, I've got the spectrum covered. Vegan food can be anything you want it to be, and with my signature *Vegan Yack Attack* stamp on it, you know it's going to awesome!

Chapter 1

ATTACK OF THE VEGAN BOWLS!

You may ask yourself, "What makes a bowl any better than other ways to eat food?" Well, for one thing, bowls are fairly well contained from a logistical perspective. Have you ever tried eating a salad off of a plate? It may be one of the messiest ways to eat something; you have to chase food around with your fork, and the last few bites are always the hardest to get. Second, some of the best foods are served in bowls! Imagine trying to chow down on some pho, or maybe crème brûlée, using a plate or saucer. Both of those situations sound like they could be a form of punishment. Last, bowls are a fun way to take a few foods or ingredients that you love—and that may not hold their own on a plate—and put them together in an incredibly tasty and colorful fashion.

But before we dive into the bowls themselves, let's first make sure we're all on the same page with the basics.

BOWL BASICS

Creating bowls is an easy task. You've probably even made bowls inadvertently while getting rid of leftovers in your pantry and refrigerator. I know that I've had nights when I put together a simple bowl of steamed grains with veggies and a sauce of some sort. Simple meals are good at the end of long days when you have used up your mental capacity on everything else and food is something that has to happen but you don't want to think too hard about it. Luckily, I have put together these amazing bowl recipes—some quicker than others—so that you don't have to make your exhausted brain work on yet one more thing.

MASTER FORMULAS

There are a couple of good formulas for putting together a stellar bowl, aside from just following the recipes in this book straight-up. One of the easiest ways to come up with ideas is to think of dishes that you already love. Sometimes taking an old favorite—such as tacos or burgers—and transforming it into a bowl turns out to be time-saving and less messy, and it gives you the option of trying all the flavors together or eating each component one at a time.

Another way of figuring out what ingredients to use in a bowl is to make it an equation (and, unlike boring math, this will end up delicious and awesome):

1. **Start with the base of the bowl. This could be any kind of grain, such as quinoa, brown rice, oats, barley, or others. Other foods that fall into this realm are pasta (whether it be gluten-free, whole wheat, or even made from zucchini), polenta, and even sliced-up tortillas.**

2. **Next, think of vegetables that you love. We are talking sweet potatoes, broccoli, Brussels sprouts, green beans, kale, and the like. Choose a few veggies that sound like they would be good together and cook 'em up. You can even group them together by types of veggies. Take, for example, Mean Green Ramen (page 104) or Roasted Root Vegetables with Smoky Tahini Sauce (page 131). If you're thinking of making a sweeter bowl, perhaps for breakfast or dessert, you may want to forgo vegetables and add your favorite fruits. You could go tropical, for example, with a pineapple, mango, and banana combination, as in Tropical Chia Pudding (page 30). Or maybe it's spring, so a berry medley makes the most sense, which would pair great with a creamy base such as oatmeal.**

3. **Although the protein part of the formula is mostly applicable to entrée bowls, it doesn't hurt to add it to other types of bowls. Keep in mind that almost all foods have protein in them; it's the amounts that vary. Even 1 cup (71 g) of chopped broccoli has 3 grams of protein! Easy-to-prepare vegan foods that up the amount of protein in any bowl are legumes, nuts, seeds, tempeh, tofu, edamame, and peas. You can season these like you would any other form of protein. For example, I love using Mexican-style spices such as chili powder, cumin, and paprika to add flavor to ground tempeh, tofu, or black beans.**

Another way to add protein is to make a tasty sauce using nuts or silken tofu. Sauces are very important to bowls because they add a different texture and a flavor explosion that can tie everything together. I don't know about you, but I consider myself a condiment queen and enjoy trying out new sauces or even sauce combinations all the time. Now, your sauce does not necessarily need to be protein-centric. Here is where a blender comes in handy! Purée bell peppers, pulse together a salsa, or whip together a homemade ranch sauce (page 192). The sky's the limit when it comes to making sauces.

4. **The next step is to add a little healthy fat into your life. You will notice that some foods cross over a few different categories, so use your discretion when deciding how many of each type to use. Go-to healthy fats for bowls include avocado, cold-pressed or extra-virgin oils, coconut foods, cacao nibs, olives, and nut or seed butters.**

5. **Now for my favorite part of making a bowl: the plating. You can neatly organize the components and add a little drizzle of sauce and a garnish, or mix them up with no rhyme or reason other than to get every different flavor in every bite. Some dishes end up being self-explanatory in terms of serving and others not so much. But don't worry—no one will judge you if you don't follow plating protocol. Just do what feels right!**

SPREADING VEGAN BOWL LOVE

I became a vegan during my first full year out of college. Working full-time, I had a more rigid schedule than in school, so I had to start planning what to eat each day. At first, I survived almost exclusively on "healthy" frozen meals, but costs started adding up, and fast! After a few months, I decided that I wanted to get into cooking food for myself.

I spent a lot of time visiting online recipe sites and occasionally making more involved non-vegan meals, and then I started researching food in depth. This wasn't too weird for me because sustainability is something that has been ingrained in my thinking patterns for a long time. So when I started learning about the damage that factory farming does to our planet, I had to seriously rethink this meat-eating thing.

Next, I started learning about the antibiotics and hormones used in farming animals and producing dairy and egg products. After that, it was hard to ignore everything that I had researched for months. I had to go vegan. For the first couple of months, I remained a vegetarian, occasionally having dairy or eggs, but one day I thought to myself, "If you don't want the antibiotics or hormones that are in meat in your body, how can you continue to eat these other animal products?" I realized that I was being a hypocrite and gave them up for good.

A few months later, I connected with the animal-compassion side of my new lifestyle. This trio of the benefits of veganism has helped me to be a more well-rounded vegan and person in general. I've happily been a vegan for five years now.

I have had some great conversations about veganism with people and some not-so-great ones, too. But I find that nothing makes a believer out of people more than putting a beautiful and delicious dish in front of them that does not have any animal products in it.

One of my favorite reactions is, "Wow! This is so good!" and usually my response is, "Right? Can you believe that I don't eat just grass and dirt all day?" (Of course, this is something that I would only say to people I know, but the sentiment rings true.) I love to bring vegan cookies or appetizers to gatherings of friends and family. Many people just don't realize how awesome and fun cruelty-free food can be.

And that's exactly where these bowls come into play! This book offers a wide variety of bowls for every palate preference, whether you are into comfort food, eating light, trying out new flavors, or just in need of something delicious and satiating. Invite some of your close ones over and chow down on recipes that won't disappoint!

Chapter 2

BOUNTIFUL BREAKFAST BOWLS

A NEW TWIST ON MORNING CLASSICS

Getting out of bed is not awesome, so why make it any harder? Here we have a few of your favorite breakfast dishes, but remade with bowl-tastic innovation. From the simple to the more involved, your morning hunger is sure to be hushed.

Chai Waffle Stick Dippers	17
Caramel Apple Slices	18
Apple Pie Smoothie Bowl	20
Peanut Butter Pretzel Oatmeal	21
Sesame Apricot Granola	22
Loaded Potato Breakfast Bowl	23
Scramble Burrito Bowl	27
Mini-Cinni Rolls with Cashew Cream Cheese Drizzle	28
Tropical Chia Pudding	30
Fruit-Stuffed Sweet Potato	31
Biscuit Nacho Bowl	33
Melon Madness Bowl	34
Nectarine Quinoa Porridge	35
Tempeh Bacon Hollandaise Bowl	36
Zebra Crepe Bowl	39
Neapolitan Smoothie Bowl	40

CHAI WAFFLE STICK DIPPERS

SOY-FREE • NUT-FREE

Waffles are a quintessential brunch food that many people love. I always saw waffles as a special weekend meal that I enjoyed far too little. Now, you can take the awesomeness of waffles and turn them into a fun finger food, filled with chai spices and dipped into maple butter. Wins all around!

To make the waffle sticks: Place all of the waffle ingredients in a blender and purée until combined and smooth. Let the mixture thicken for 10 minutes.

Preheat a Belgian waffle maker according to the manufacturer's instructions. Fill with batter and cook for 10 minutes or until the steam stops coming out (and if you have a newer waffle maker, the light turns green). Repeat until the batter is used up. If you like, keep the cooked waffles warm in a low oven while you make the remaining ones.

To make the maple butter dip: While the waffles are cooking, whisk the butter, maple syrup, and cinnamon together in a bowl and then separate the dip among 4 small bowls for serving.

When the waffles are done, cut them into strips with a serrated knife and serve with the dip.

YIELD: 4 servings

FOR THE WAFFLE STICKS:

¾ cup (175 ml) orange juice

¾ cup (175 ml) unsweetened nondairy, soy-free, nut-free milk

1 tablespoon (15 ml) olive oil

1 teaspoon vanilla extract

1¼ cups (156 g) unbleached all-purpose flour

½ cup (40 g) rolled oats

2 tablespoons (24 g) organic cane sugar

2 teaspoons baking powder

1½ teaspoons ground cinnamon

¾ teaspoon ground ginger

½ teaspoon ground cardamom

½ teaspoon ground allspice

½ teaspoon ground cloves

FOR THE MAPLE BUTTER DIP:

¼ cup (55 g) soy-free vegan butter, melted

⅓ cup (80 ml) maple syrup

¼ teaspoon ground cinnamon

CARAMEL APPLE SLICES

GLUTEN-FREE • SOY-FREE

When my sister and I were kids, one of our favorite snacks was the pairing of green apple wedges with a tub of microwaveable caramel. Boy, have we come a long way! Here we have a much healthier version with nearly raw Date Caramel and add-ins such as bananas, peanuts, and dried cranberries.

Core each apple and thinly slice them to create "chips." As you cut, soak the slices in a large bowl filled with the water and lemon juice to prevent browning.

Once you are ready to serve, drain the apple slices and pat dry with a clean towel. Divide the apples among 4 bowls, drizzle the Date Caramel over each one, and top each with banana slices, peanuts, chocolate chips, and dried cranberries. Serve immediately.

YIELD: **4 servings**

1 pound (455 g) tart apples of your choice

3 cups (700 ml) water

3 tablespoons (45 ml) lemon juice

1 recipe Date Caramel (page 200)

2 bananas, peeled and sliced

½ cup (73 g) roasted salted peanuts, chopped

¼ cup (44 g) soy-free, gluten-free vegan chocolate chips

¼ cup (30 g) dried cranberries

APPLE PIE SMOOTHIE BOWL

GLUTEN-FREE • SOY-FREE

For many people, apples mean that fall and cooler temperatures have arrived, and although the former may be the case in Southern California, temperatures still remain warm into November. With this apple pie smoothie bowl, you can celebrate the change of seasons while keeping your cool.

To make the smoothie: Place all of the ingredients in a blender in the order listed. Press the apple pieces down firmly in the pitcher, as they will create the liquid needed to purée the rest of ingredients. Blend until very smooth. If you would like a thinner consistency, add some soy-free nondairy milk. Pour into 2 bowls and store in the freezer while making the topping.

To make the pie topping: In a food processor, pulse the almonds, dates, cinnamon, and salt together until they are small chunks. Shake over the top of each smoothie bowl and serve.

YIELD: **2 servings**

FOR THE APPLE PIE SMOOTHIE:

1½ pounds (680 g) green apples, cored and chopped

2 frozen bananas, peeled

3 cups (90 g) packed fresh spinach

1 teaspoon ground cinnamon

1 teaspoon vanilla extract

Pinch of salt

2 teaspoons maca powder (optional)

Unsweetened nondairy soy-free milk (optional)

FOR THE PIE TOPPING:

¼ cup (36 g) raw almonds

¼ cup (45 g) dried dates, pitted

¼ teaspoon ground cinnamon

Pinch of salt

PEANUT BUTTER PRETZEL OATMEAL

SOY-FREE

Who else has a hard time passing by the peanut butter pretzel bins in the bulk section of the grocery store without wanting to buy bags of them? It can't only be me. The salty, crunchy snacks are a welcome addition to this breakfast of creamy oats.

In a small pot, combine the soy-free nondairy milk, water, peanut butter, maple syrup, vanilla, and rolled oats over medium heat. Bring to a boil, adjust the heat to medium-low, and simmer for 5 minutes, stirring occasionally, until the oats are fully cooked.

Stir in the salt and divide the oatmeal between 2 bowls, topping each with ¼ cup (15 g) of crushed peanut butter pretzels and a light drizzle of maple syrup, if using.

YIELD: 2 servings

1 cup (235 ml) unsweetened soy-free nondairy milk

⅓ cup (80 ml) water

¼ cup (65 g) peanut butter

3 tablespoons (45 ml) maple syrup

1 teaspoon vanilla extract

⅔ cup (53 g) rolled oats

Pinch of salt

½ cup (30 g) peanut butter pretzels, broken into smaller pieces

Maple syrup, for serving (optional)

SESAME APRICOT GRANOLA

GLUTEN-FREE • SOY-FREE

This recipe started off as a bit of a fluke some time ago, and it has now become my favorite granola! Tahini does a great job of clumping the grains, seeds, and dried apricots together, and when combined with maple, cardamom, and coconut, it is all taken to the next level of granola greatness.

Preheat oven to 350°F (180°C, or gas mark 4) and line a baking sheet with a silicone baking mat or parchment paper.

In a large bowl, combine the rolled oats, coconut flakes, buckwheat groats, almonds, apricots, chia seeds, sesame seeds, cardamom, and salt. In a smaller bowl, whisk together the tahini, maple syrup, and vanilla.

Add the wet mixture to the dry mixture and fold together until evenly coated. Spread the granola out over the lined baking sheet and bake for 10 minutes, stirring it around halfway through. Transfer it to a cooling rack for 5 minutes before eating or storing for later. This granola tastes great on plain coconut milk yogurt with a light drizzle of maple syrup or agave nectar.

YIELD: 6 servings

½ cup (48 g) gluten-free rolled oats

½ cup (30 g) unsweetened large coconut flakes

½ cup (92 g) raw buckwheat groats

½ cup (50 g) raw almonds, chopped

½ cup (26 g) dried apricots, diced

2 tablespoons (30 g) chia seeds

2 tablespoons (16 g) sesame seeds

¼ teaspoon ground cardamom

⅛ teaspoon salt

¼ cup (60 g) tahini

3 to 4 tablespoons (45 to 60 ml) maple syrup, or preferred sweetness

1 teaspoon vanilla extract

LOADED POTATO BREAKFAST BOWL

GLUTEN-FREE • SUGAR-FREE

This crispy potato hash is covered in Heavenly mushroom gravy, and it is the perfect breakfast food to serve your dad. I know firsthand that this bowl is a crowd-pleaser!

To make the potato hash: Melt the coconut oil in a large pan over medium-high heat. When the pan is hot enough to make water sizzle, put the potatoes in. Cover and cook for 15 minutes, stirring occasionally. (Start your gravy now, if you can.)

Add the onions to the potatoes, cover, and sauté until the onions become translucent. Lower the heat to medium and then add the tomatoes and bell pepper to the pan. Leave uncovered and sauté until the potatoes are crispy and cooked all the way through.

Season the hash with salt and pepper. Wait until right before serving to fold in the arugula, so that it does not become too limp.

To make the mushroom gravy: Make the gravy at the same time as the potatoes if you can; I wouldn't recommend doing it afterward, as the potatoes may get mushy when reheated.

Coat a medium saucepan with 1 tablespoon (15 ml) of the coconut milk. Bring to a simmer over medium heat. Next, add the onion and sauté for 2 minutes and then stir in the garlic. Cook until the onions are almost translucent and then add the mushrooms. Sauté until the mushrooms have darkened and reduced in size.

Sprinkle the cornstarch over the onion-mushroom mixture and stir until everything is coated evenly. Put the contents of the saucepan in a blender or food processor along with the remaining coconut milk, the nutritional yeast, and liquid aminos and pulse a few times for a smoother consistency.

(continued on next page)

FOR THE POTATO HASH:

2 teaspoons coconut oil

1½ pounds (680 g) russet potatoes, chopped

1 cup (160 g) diced white onion

1 cup (180 g) diced tomato

½ cup (75 g) diced red bell pepper

Salt and freshly ground black pepper, to taste

1 cup (20 g) firmly packed arugula

FOR THE MUSHROOM GRAVY:

1½ cups (355 ml) plus 1 tablespoon (15 ml) light coconut milk, divided

½ cup (80 g) diced white onion

2 cloves of garlic, minced

½ cup (35 g) diced baby bella mushrooms

1 tablespoon (8 g) cornstarch

3 tablespoons (12 g) nutritional yeast

1 tablespoon (15 ml) liquid aminos

Freshly ground black pepper, to taste

Vegan cheese shreds, for topping (optional)

(continued from previous page)

Pour the gravy back into the saucepan and bring to a boil. Lower the heat so that the gravy simmers. Stir or whisk every couple of minutes until it reaches the desired thickness and then season with pepper.

Divide the potato hash among 4 bowls (don't forget to fold in the arugula first!) and top with cheese shreds, if using, and the gravy. Serve immediately.

YIELD: **2 large or 4 small servings**

SCRAMBLE BURRITO BOWL

GLUTEN-FREE • NUT-FREE • SUGAR-FREE

My high school had a surf team as part of its sports roster, and I was on it. After a good season, the coaches would take us out for breakfast burritos. This bowl has everything that a great breakfast burrito would have, just without the massive tortilla that could blow apart at any moment.

To make the tofu scramble and fajita veggies: In a large, cast-iron skillet, warm the oil over medium heat. Once hot, use your hands to break the tofu apart into large crumbles into the skillet. Brown the tofu for 2 to 3 minutes and then stir it around to brown the other sides. You want it to have a light brown crust on a couple of sides.

Next, adjust the heat to medium-low and stir in the nutritional yeast, turmeric, and Indian black salt until the scramble is evenly coated. Season with salt and pepper, and push the scramble to one side of the skillet.

Place the red onion and bell peppers into the other half of the skillet and sauté until the onions become translucent. Add the black beans and spinach, cook until the spinach has wilted, and season with salt and pepper.

To assemble: Divide the scramble and fajita veggies between 2 bowls. Top with the salsa, avocado, and cilantro and serve.

YIELD: 2 servings

FOR THE TOFU SCRAMBLE:

2 tablespoons (28 ml) mild-flavored cooking oil

1 package (12 ounces, or 340 g) extra-firm tofu, drained

2 tablespoons (6 g) nutritional yeast

Pinch of ground turmeric

½ teaspoon Indian black salt (kala namak)

Salt and freshly ground black pepper, to taste

FOR THE FAJITA VEGGIES:

¾ cup (120 g) half-moon slices of red onion

1 cup (150 g) bell pepper strips (any color)

½ cup (120 g) cooked black beans

2 cups (60 g) packed baby spinach

Salt and freshly ground black pepper, to taste

FOR THE ASSEMBLY:

¼ cup (65 g) Roasted Chipotle Salsa (page 46)

¼ cup (37 g) peeled, pitted, and diced avocado

2 tablespoons (2 g) fresh cilantro

MINI-CINNI ROLLS WITH CASHEW CREAM CHEESE DRIZZLE

SOY-FREE

I have always felt that smaller versions of your favorite foods taste better. Is it because they are cuter? Possibly. Now you can enjoy an irresistible bowl of sweet, cinnamon-y rolls covered in the best cashew cream cheese drizzle this side of ever.

To make the mini-cinni rolls: Combine the warm water, 1 tablespoon (12 g) of the sugar, and the active dry yeast together in a bowl and let sit for 15 minutes for the yeast to proof.

In a large bowl, sift the all-purpose flour, pastry flour, and salt together. Once the yeast has bubbled up, stir the olive oil and vanilla into the yeast mixture and add the wet mixture to the dry mixture. Knead for 3 to 5 minutes until the dough is smooth and pliable. If it's too sticky, add a little flour and knead; if too dry, add a drizzle of oil.

Form the dough into a ball, put it into an oiled bowl, cover with a towel, and let rise for 45 minutes. When the dough has almost doubled in size, knead it for 1 minute and roll it out into a ¼-inch (6 mm)-thick rectangle, about 6 x 16 inches (15 x 40 cm).

Whisk the coconut oil, maple syrup, remaining 1½ tablespoons (18 g) sugar, and cinnamon together in a small bowl and then spread it onto the dough in an even layer. Carefully roll the dough up, starting from the long side, rolling tightly, pinching the seam together and smoothing the edge out. You should end up with a roll about 18 inches (46 cm) long. Slice the roll into pieces about ¾ inch (2 cm) thick to get 24 mini rolls.

Grease a 5 x 9-inch (13 x 23 cm) baking dish, arrange the rolls in the dish cut side up, and let rise for 30 minutes or until they fill the baking dish. Meanwhile, preheat the oven to 350°F (180°C, or gas mark 4).

FOR THE MINI-CINNI ROLLS:

½ cup (120 ml) warm water

2½ tablespoons (30 g) organic cane sugar, divided

1 packet (0.25 ounce, or 7 g) active dry yeast

1¼ cups (156 g) unbleached all-purpose flour

⅓ cup (40 g) whole wheat pastry flour

⅛ teaspoon salt

2 tablespoons (28 ml) olive oil

½ teaspoon vanilla extract

2 tablespoons (28 g) coconut oil, melted

2 tablespoons (28 ml) maple syrup

1 tablespoon (7 g) ground cinnamon

Bake the rolls for 15 to 17 minutes until the tops have turned golden brown. Transfer the baking dish to a cooling rack.

To make the cashew cream cheese drizzle: Place all of the ingredients in a blender and purée until velvety smooth. Taste and add more agave if you would prefer a sweeter drizzle. Refrigerate the drizzle for about 10 minutes to let it thicken.

Divide the mini-cinnis among 4 bowls, top with the cashew cream cheese drizzle, and serve.

YIELD: 4 servings

FOR THE CASHEW CREAM CHEESE DRIZZLE:

½ cup (56 g) raw cashews

¼ cup (60 ml) water, plus more if necessary

3 tablespoons (26 g) plain vegan yogurt

3 tablespoons (45 ml) agave nectar

1 tablespoon (14 g) coconut oil

TROPICAL CHIA PUDDING

GLUTEN-FREE • SOY-FREE

Chia puddings are a fantastic way to incorporate fiber and protein into your diet first thing in the morning. Filled with delicious tropical fruits—pineapple, mango, and kiwi—this pudding is sure to start your day off with daydreams of island beaches.

In a large bowl, whisk together the water, coconut milk, orange juice, agave nectar, orange zest, chia seeds, and salt. Set in the refrigerator for at least 1 hour, stirring halfway through; you can also soak the seeds overnight.

Fold half of the mango, pineapple, and kiwi into the pudding and then divide among 4 bowls. Top with the remaining fruit and the shredded coconut and serve.

YIELD: 4 servings

1 cup (235 ml) water

¾ cup (180 ml) full-fat coconut milk

¼ cup (60 ml) orange juice

2 to 3 tablespoons (30 to 45 ml) agave nectar

1 teaspoon grated orange zest

¾ cup (180 g) chia seeds

Pinch of salt

1 cup (175 g) peeled, seeded, and chopped mango

1 cup (181 g) peeled and diced pineapple

1 cup (178 g) peeled and diced kiwi

2 tablespoons (15 g) unsweetened shredded coconut

FRUIT-STUFFED SWEET POTATO

GLUTEN-FREE • SOY-FREE

Sweet potatoes are great on their own, but filling them with seasonal winter fruit and topping them off with a maple-tahini sauce turns them into an even better breakfast.

To make the stuffed sweet potatoes: Preheat the oven to 375°F (190°C, or gas mark 5). Wrap the sweet potatoes individually in aluminum foil and place them on a baking sheet. Bake for 30 minutes or until fork-tender.

In a large bowl, combine the pears, figs, cranberries, and walnuts. When the potatoes are done, let them cool for 10 minutes before unwrapping the foil and cutting them in half lengthwise. Divide the fruit filling among the potatoes, mounding it on top of the potato halves. Arrange them on the baking sheet and place them back in the oven to bake for 15 minutes.

To make the maple-tahini sauce: Whisk all of the ingredients together in a small bowl, drizzle over the tops of the baked sweet potatoes, and serve.

YIELD: 4 servings

FOR THE STUFFED SWEET POTATOES:

4 sweet potatoes (½ pound or 225 g each)

½ pound (225 g) pears, cored and chopped

½ pound (225 g) fresh figs, sliced in half

3 ounces (85 g) fresh cranberries (or thawed frozen)

½ cup (60 g) walnuts, chopped

FOR THE MAPLE-TAHINI SAUCE:

3 tablespoons (45 g) tahini

2 tablespoons (28 ml) maple syrup

1 tablespoon (15 ml) water

1 teaspoon vanilla extract

Pinch of salt

BISCUIT NACHO BOWL

SOY-FREE OPTION • SUGAR-FREE

In Austin, Texas, there is a food trailer that offers up a dish of biscuits and gravy, but with the addition of some Southwestern toppings, and it looks amazing. I take it to the next Tex-Mex level by dousing fluffy spiced biscuits with a homemade nacho cheese sauce and all of your standard nacho accoutrements.

To make the biscuits: Preheat the oven to 450°F (230°C, or gas mark 8) and line a baking sheet with parchment paper.

In a large bowl, sift the all-purpose flour, pastry flour, baking powder, cumin, salt, chili powder, and black pepper together. Use a pastry cutter to cut the coconut oil into the flour until it is crumbly. Add the onion and soy-free nondairy milk and fold together until everything is combined. Do not overmix.

Dust your work surface with flour and roll the dough out to 1 inch (2.5 cm) thick. Using a biscuit cutter, cut the dough into 8 biscuits and place them on the baking sheet. Give them a light coat of cooking oil spray and bake for 12 to 13 minutes until the tops are golden.

To make the cheeze sauce: In a small pot over medium-low heat, combine the Cheezy Cheddar Sauce, pickled jalapeño juice, pickled jalapeños, smoked paprika, and cayenne. Bring to a simmer, stirring occasionally, and then turn heat to low to keep the warm.

To assemble: Split each biscuit in half. Place 4 biscuit halves in each of the serving bowls, cover them with nacho cheeze sauce, and top each bowl with your choice of black olives, jalapeños, Silky Sour Cream, Simple Guacamole, Roasted Chipotle Salsa, and diced scallions. Serve hot.

Note: To make this recipe soy-free, omit the Silky Sour Cream.

YIELD: 4 servings

FOR THE BISCUITS:

1½ cups (188 g) unbleached all-purpose flour

1 cup (120 g) whole wheat pastry flour

1 tablespoon (14 g) baking powder

1 teaspoon ground cumin

1½ teaspoons salt

½ teaspoon chili powder

¼ teaspoon freshly ground black pepper

⅔ cup (150 g) refined coconut oil

3 tablespoons (30 g) diced white onion

7 ounces (200 ml) unsweetened soy-free nondairy milk

Cooking oil spray

FOR THE CHEEZE SAUCE:

1 batch of Cheezy Cheddar Sauce (page 194)

¼ cup (60 ml) pickled jalapeño juice (the liquid from the pickled jalapeños)

2 tablespoons (18 g) diced pickled jalapeños

½ teaspoon smoked paprika

¼ teaspoon cayenne pepper

FOR THE ASSEMBLY:

¼ cup (35 g) sliced black olives

¼ cup (23 g) sliced fresh jalapeños

¼ cup (60 g) Silky Sour Cream (page 194)

¼ cup (56 g) Simple Guacamole (page 198)

¼ cup (65 g) Roasted Chipotle Salsa (page 46)

2 tablespoons (12 g) diced scallions

MELON MADNESS BOWL

GLUTEN-FREE • SOY-FREE • NUT-FREE • SUGAR-FREE

While driving through Los Angeles, you are bound to come across one of the thousands of fresh fruit carts that are parked on various street corners. One of the foods they offer at these carts is a mixed fruit cup with a side of zesty chili powder shake. Improving upon this treat, we have here a flavorful melon breakfast with added spice and wholesome hemp seeds.

In a large bowl, toss the honeydew, cantaloupe, and watermelon balls with the lime juice, lime zest, chili powder, cayenne pepper, and salt. Chill in the refrigerator for 30 minutes.

   Divide among 4 bowls, sprinkle the hemp seeds over the top of each, and serve.

YIELD: 4 servings

1 pound (455 g) honeydew melon, scooped into balls

1 pound (455 g) cantaloupe, scooped into balls

1 pound (455 g) watermelon, scooped into balls

2 tablespoons (28 ml) lime juice

½ teaspoon grated lime zest

½ teaspoon chili powder

¼ teaspoon cayenne pepper

¼ teaspoon salt

¼ cup (37 g) hulled hemp seeds

NECTARINE QUINOA PORRIDGE

GLUTEN-FREE • SOY-FREE

Comforting porridge does not always have to be made with oats. Instead, try enjoying protein-rich quinoa topped with warm nectarines for a breakfast change-up.

In a medium pot over medium heat, stir together 1½ cups (255 g) of the nectarines, the quinoa, soy-free nondairy milk, coconut sugar, and vanilla, and then bring to a boil. Adjust the heat to medium-low and simmer, partially covered, for 25 minutes or until the quinoa is cooked through, stirring occasionally.

Divide the quinoa between 2 bowls, top each with ½ cup (85 g) of the remaining sliced nectarines and half of the pistachios and serve.

YIELD: **2 servings**

1½ cups (255 g) plus 1 cup (170 g) sliced nectarines, divided

⅔ cup (116 g) quinoa, rinsed and drained

⅔ cup (160 ml) unsweetened nondairy milk

3 tablespoons (27 g) coconut sugar

1½ teaspoons vanilla extract

¼ cup (31 g) roasted shelled pistachios

Make this recipe in every season by substituting nectarines with mixed berries in the spring, persimmons in the fall, and cranberries in the winter.

TEMPEH BACON HOLLANDAISE BOWL

GLUTEN-FREE

This bowl has smoky, sweet tempeh bacon, eggy tofu, sautéed asparagus, peppery arugula, and fresh tomatoes, all covered in an insanely good hollandaise sauce. Need I say more?

To make the hollandaise sauce: Place all of the ingredients in a blender and purée until smooth. Transfer the sauce to a large sauté pan and bring to a simmer over medium-low heat, whisking frequently. Continue whisking and cook until the sauce has thickened and is no longer grainy from the chickpea flour. Adjust the heat to low to keep warm for serving.

To make the tofu eggs: Slice the tofu in half lengthwise and then into 8 triangles. In a small bowl, whisk the nutritional yeast, Indian black salt, regular salt, and black pepper together. Dust each side of the tofu with this mixture.

In a large pan, warm the coconut oil over medium heat. Once hot, place the tofu triangles in the pan and brown both sides for 5 minutes each. Adjust the heat to medium-low and move the tofu to one side of the pan.

To assemble: Place the asparagus pieces in the other side of the hot pan and cook for 5 to 6 minutes, stirring occasionally. Season with salt and pepper and divide the asparagus among 4 bowls.

Place 2 pieces of tofu in each bowl, along with ½ cup (10 g) of the arugula. Divide the Tempting Tempeh Bacon and tomatoes among the bowls and drizzle each with hollandaise sauce. Serve immediately.

YIELD: 4 servings

FOR THE HOLLANDAISE SAUCE:

¼ cup (30 g) chickpea flour

1 cup (235 ml) water

¼ cup (55 g) vegan butter, melted

1 tablespoon (4 g) nutritional yeast

2 teaspoons lemon juice

¾ teaspoon Indian black salt (kala namak)

¼ teaspoon ground turmeric

¼ teaspoon sea salt

FOR THE TOFU EGGS:

1 package (12 ounces, or 340 g) extra-firm tofu, drained

2 teaspoons nutritional yeast

¼ teaspoon Indian black salt (kala namak)

Pinch each of of salt and freshly ground black pepper

1½ teaspoons coconut oil

FOR THE ASSEMBLY:

½ pound (225 g) asparagus spears, cut in half with woody stems removed

Salt and freshly ground black pepper, to taste

2 cups (40 g) packed baby arugula

1 batch of Tempting Tempeh Bacon (page 197)

½ pound (225 g) tomatoes, sliced into wedges

ZEBRA CREPE BOWL

SOY-FREE

This dish blossomed from having more crepes than filling for breakfast one morning. I saved the crepes for later and then baked them into bowls and ate ice cream out of them! These bowls, with their fresh fruits, are more appropriate for breakfast. The zebra stripes of chocolate and vanilla sauce keep them a little decadent.

To make the crepe bowls: Preheat the oven to 350°F (180°C, or gas mark 4). In a small bowl, sift together the flour, sugar, and salt, and then stir in the soy-free nondairy milk, melted coconut oil, and maple syrup until there are no lumps in the batter.

Place the bowl in the freezer for 20 minutes. Lightly grease the underside of 4 small ovenproof bowls (you will use these to mold the cooked crepes). After the batter is done setting, warm a griddle or large skillet over medium-low heat and spray with a thin coat of oil. Pour 2 tablespoons (28 ml) of the batter into the center of the griddle, pick it up, and tilt the pan in circles to spread out the batter to about 7 inches (18 cm) in diameter.

Cook the crepe on one side for 2 to 3 minutes, and then carefully flip it over and cook it for an additional 2 minutes. Remove from the skillet and drape it, centered, over the overturned bowl. Repeat for the remaining 3 crepes and then place the bowls on a baking sheet and put in the oven for 10 to 12 minutes until the edges start to brown. Transfer the baking sheet with the bowls to a cooling rack to cool for 15 to 20 minutes.

To make the filling: In a large bowl, toss all of the berries together.

To assemble: Carefully separate the crepe bowls from the bowls, set on serving plates or in larger bowls, and divide the berry mixture among them. Drizzle each one with Chocolate Sauce and Sweet Cashew Cream, top with pecans, and serve.

YIELD: 4 servings

FOR THE CREPE BOWLS:

½ cup (63 g) unbleached all-purpose flour

1½ teaspoons organic cane sugar

⅛ teaspoon salt

½ cup plus 2 tablespoons (150 ml) unsweetened soy-free nondairy milk

1 tablespoon (14 g) coconut oil, melted

1 tablespoon (15 ml) maple syrup

FOR THE FILLING:

½ pound (225 g) fresh strawberries, chopped

¼ pound (115 g) fresh blueberries

¼ pound (115 g) fresh blackberries

FOR THE ASSEMBLY:

1 batch Chocolate Sauce (page 199)

1 batch of Sweet Cashew Cream (page 200)

¼ cup (28 g) chopped pecans

NEAPOLITAN SMOOTHIE BOWL

GLUTEN-FREE • SOY-FREE • NUT-FREE • SUGAR-FREE

Who says you can't have ice cream for breakfast? Make this healthy smoothie bowl to get a frosty taste of rich chocolate, creamy vanilla, and tart strawberry layers, topped with fresh fruit and crunchy cacao nibs. You can prep the chocolate and vanilla layers the night before and just finish with the strawberry layer and garnishes in the morning.

To make the chocolate layer: Place all of the ingredients in a blender and purée until smooth. Divide between 2 bowls and place them in the freezer until set, about 30 minutes.

To make the vanilla layer: Place all of the ingredients in a blender and purée until smooth. Divide between the 2 bowls and place them in the freezer until set, about 30 minutes (or overnight if you are prepping the night before).

To make the strawberry layer: Place all of the ingredients in a blender and purée until smooth. Divide between the 2 bowls.

Finishing touches: Top each smoothie bowl with sliced strawberries, sliced bananas, cacao nibs, and hemp seeds. Serve immediately.

YIELD: 2 servings

> Soak your dates in warm water for 15 minutes before making this recipe so that they blend more smoothly.

FOR THE CHOCOLATE LAYER:

1 cup (252 g) frozen
banana pieces

3 tablespoons (15 g) raw
cacao powder

4 Medjool dates, pitted

Pinch of salt

⅓ cup (80 ml) water

FOR THE VANILLA LAYER:

1½ cups (378 g) frozen
banana pieces

¼ cup (37 g) hulled hemp seeds

3 Medjool dates, pitted

Seeds scraped from ½ of
a vanilla bean

Pinch of salt

⅓ cup (80 ml) water

FOR THE STRAWBERRY LAYER:

1½ cups (382 g) frozen
strawberries

3 Medjool dates, pitted

½ cup (120 ml) water

1 tablespoon (15 ml) lemon juice

FOR THE FINISHING TOUCHES:

½ cup (85 g) sliced fresh
strawberries

½ cup (75 g) sliced fresh bananas

2 tablespoons (16 g) cacao nibs

2 tablespoons (18 g) hulled
hemp seeds

WHITE BEAN BEER FONDUE

GLUTEN-FREE OPTION • SOY-FREE • SUGAR-FREE

Fondue makes for a fun appetizer to be shared among friends, whether for a dinner party or a game night. This creamy, low-fat fondue is a delicious crowd-pleaser, especially with its beer-tinged aroma.

To make the fondue: Drain and rinse the cashews and then place them in a blender along with the white beans (plus the liquid from the beans), soy-free non-dairy milk, beer, nutritional yeast, tapioca starch, garlic, both vinegars, and mustard. Purée the mixture until very smooth and transfer the cheese sauce to a large saucepan.

Bring the mixture to a simmer over medium heat, whisking frequently to make sure the bottom doesn't burn. The fondue will thicken, and you want it to get hot so that the tapioca starch completely dissolves. Whisk until the fondue leaves a thick coating of sauce on the whisk or a spoon when dipped into it. Add the salt and stir.

Transfer the fondue to a small slow cooker, fondue pot, or glass bowl for serving. Place the broccoli, carrot sticks, toast cubes, apple, and pretzels on a serving tray with skewers for dipping.

YIELD: 4 servings

FOR THE FONDUE:

¼ cup (35 g) raw cashews, soaked in warm water for 30 minutes

1 can (15 ounces, or 425 g) white beans, undrained

½ cup (120 ml) unsweetened soy-free nondairy milk

½ cup (120 ml) ale or lager (gluten-free, if necessary)

¼ cup (15 g) nutritional yeast

2 tablespoons (15 g) tapioca starch

2 cloves of garlic, peeled

2 teaspoons coconut vinegar

1 teaspoon apple cider vinegar

1 teaspoon Dijon mustard

1 teaspoon salt

FOR DIPPING:

1½ cups (107 g) broccoli florets

1½ cups (195 g) carrot sticks

1½ cups (75 g) toasted cubed bread (gluten-free, if necessary)

1 cup (150 g) cubed green apple

1 cup (60 g) pretzels (gluten-free, if necessary)

SPICY SESAME BRUSSELS BITES

GLUTEN-FREE • NUT-FREE

Brussels sprouts are the vegetable that your mom used to completely overcook for holidays—which made everyone hate them—but that are now making a comeback in a huge way. There's just something about these "mini-cabbages," as I call them, which makes them my favorite choice for roasting and serving to the masses.

Preheat the oven to 375°F (190°C, or gas mark 5) and line a baking sheet with parchment paper. In a large bowl, toss together the Brussels sprouts, sesame oil, red pepper flakes, salt, and ginger. Spread the sprouts out on the lined baking sheet.

Bake for 25 minutes, stirring halfway through so that the sprouts roast evenly. Once roasted, place them back in the large bowl and toss them with the rice vinegar, agave nectar, toasted sesame seeds, and liquid aminos. Serve hot.

YIELD: 4 small servings

1½ pounds (680 g) Brussels sprouts, trimmed but kept whole

2 tablespoons (28 ml) toasted sesame oil

1 teaspoon crushed red pepper flakes

¼ teaspoon salt

⅛ teaspoon ground ginger

1 tablespoon (15 ml) rice vinegar

1 tablespoon (15 ml) agave nectar

2 teaspoons sesame seeds, toasted

1 teaspoon liquid aminos or tamari

ROASTED CHIPOTLE SALSA

GLUTEN-FREE • SOY-FREE • NUT-FREE • SUGAR-FREE

There is no reason to resort to mediocre store-bought salsas when you can make a better version at home. Fuel your chip addiction with this restaurant-style salsa, made up of roasted tomatoes, smoky chipotle chile powder, and fresh lime juice.

Prepare a hot fire in a grill (350°F, or 180°C) and oil the grill grates. Grill the tomatoes and jalapeños until charred on all sides. Remove them from the grill, place on a plate, and cover with a larger plate or a bowl.

2 pounds (910 g) tomatoes

2 ounces (55 g) fresh jalapeños

½ cup (80 g) chopped red onion

¼ cup (4 g) fresh cilantro

1 teaspoon lime juice

½ teaspoon ground chipotle chile powder

½ teaspoon salt, or to taste

(continued on next page)

(continued from previous page)

After about 15 minutes, peel the skins off the tomatoes and jalapeños and remove the stems (for less spicy heat, remove the seeds also). Place them in a food processor with the red onion, cilantro, lime juice, chipotle chile powder, and salt and then pulse until slightly chunky.

Transfer the salsa to a large jar and refrigerate for at least 1 hour before serving. The salsa will keep for up to 2 weeks in the refrigerator.

YIELD: 8 servings

BUFFALO JACKFRUIT DIP

GLUTEN-FREE

My mom used to make a buffalo chicken dip similar to this one in my pre-vegan days. When I first learned about jackfruit, re-creating her creamy, indulgent dip, but in a healthier way, immediately came to my mind. I added some spinach to lighten it up. Serve this addicting dip at your next party—it will be hard to resist!

Preheat the oven to 350°F (180°C, or gas mark 4).

Shred the jackfruit by hand into a large bowl. Add the vegan cream cheese, Cheezy Cheddar Sauce, Irresistible Ranch Dressing, and hot sauce and mix until combined. Fold in the spinach until combined and then spoon the mixture into an 8- or 9-inch (20 or 23 cm) round baking dish.

Bake the dip for 30 minutes or until it is hot in the center and bubbling around the edges. Transfer to a cooling rack to cool for 5 minutes. Garnish with the scallions. Serve warm with chips and/or cut-up veggies.

YIELD: 8 servings

1 can (20 ounces, or 560 g) jackfruit, drained

1 container (8 ounces, or 225 g) vegan cream cheese

¾ cup (161 g) Cheezy Cheddar Sauce (page 194)

½ cup (120 g) Irresistible Ranch Dressing (page 192)

¼ cup (60 ml) hot sauce (Tabasco, Frank's RedHot, or similar)

3 cups (90 g) packed baby spinach

2 tablespoons (12 g) diced scallions

Chips or sliced veggies of your choice, for serving

PLANTAIN TOTS CON MOJO

GLUTEN-FREE • SOY-FREE • SUGAR-FREE

Not too long ago, I was working with a restaurant to help with menu development, and lucky for me it was a Puerto Rican vegan restaurant. Soon after the project started, my love for plantains grew by leaps and bounds, and I realized that I needed to put a childhood spin on one of my favorite starchy fruits. Tots it is!

To make the tots: Using a food processor grater attachment or a handheld grater, grate the plantains. Place them in a bowl with the coconut oil, gluten-free flour, and sea salt and then mash them with a fork or potato masher until the mixture is chunky but holds together.

Fill a cast-iron skillet with 1 inch (2.5 cm) of mild-flavored cooking oil and heat it to 375°F (190°C). Using about 1 tablespoon (15 g) of the plantain mixture, form cylinder shapes by pressing the mixture together. Repeat until all of the plantain mixture is used up. Place a few tots at a time into the hot oil (you should hear it sizzle and pop when you gently drop them in).

Fry the tots for 2 minutes on one side and then flip them over and fry for an additional 2 minutes until browned. Transfer the fried tots to a plate lined with paper towels to absorb excess oil. Repeat the frying process until all the tots have been fried.

To make the mojo sauce: Place the olive oil, garlic, lime juice, and salt in a blender and purée until smooth. Pour the mixture into a small saucepan and cook for 2 to 3 minutes, basically just long enough to take the edge off the raw garlic.

Place the tots in a large serving bowl and the mojo sauce in a small serving bowl and serve immediately.

YIELD: **4 servings**

FOR THE PLANTAIN TOTS:

2 pounds (910 g) green plantains, peeled

¼ cup (56 g) coconut oil

6 tablespoons (51 g) gluten-free flour

1 teaspoon sea salt

Mild-flavored cooking oil, for frying

FOR THE MOJO SAUCE:

¼ cup (60 ml) olive oil

2 cloves of garlic, peeled

¼ cup (60 ml) lime juice

⅛ teaspoon salt

MEDITERRANEAN LAYER DIP

GLUTEN-FREE • SOY-FREE • SUGAR-FREE

- -

Why choose between different types of dip to bring to a party when you can combine the creaminess of hummus with the salty, chewy texture of tapenade and finish it off with a fresh basil pesto? Serve this pretty, layered dip with pita chips or fresh vegetable spears and sticks.

- -

To make the red lentil hummus: Place the red lentils and water in a small pot and bring to a boil over high heat. Reduce the heat to medium-low and simmer the lentils until cooked, about 20 minutes. Drain any excess water.

In a food processor with an s-blade, pulse the cooked lentils with the tahini, olive oil, lemon juice, cumin, garlic, and sea salt until very smooth. Set the hummus aside and rinse out the processor.

To make the pesto: Place all of the ingredients in the food processor and pulse until mostly smooth; you may need to scrape the sides with a spatula and pulse more for an even consistency. Set the pesto aside and rinse out the processor.

To make the olive tapenade: Place all of the ingredients in the food processor and pulse until all pieces are the size of small grains; you don't want this to be as smooth as a paste.

Layer the dips in a glass bowl, starting with the hummus, then adding the pesto, and last adding the tapenade. Garnish with fresh basil leaves and serve.

YIELD: 8 servings

FOR THE RED LENTIL HUMMUS:

2/3 cup (128 g) dried red lentils

1½ cups (355 ml) water

2 tablespoons (30 g) tahini

1 tablespoon (15 ml) olive oil

1 tablespoon (15 ml) lemon juice

1 teaspoon ground cumin

1 clove of garlic, peeled

¼ to ½ teaspoon sea salt

FOR THE PESTO:

3 cups (60 g) arugula

1½ cups (60 g) fresh basil leaves, plus a few more for garnish

¼ cup (35 g) pine nuts

1 or 2 cloves of garlic, peeled

3 tablespoons (45 ml) olive oil

2 tablespoons (28 ml) lemon juice

¼ teaspoon sea salt

Freshly ground black pepper, to taste

FOR THE OLIVE TAPENADE:

½ cup (85 g) pitted black olives

½ cup (85 g) pitted green olives

1 tablespoon (8 g) capers

1 tablespoon (15 ml) lemon juice

1 clove of garlic, peeled

1 teaspoon nutritional yeast

⅛ teaspoon freshly ground black pepper

TIKKA CAULIFLOWER CHUNKS

GLUTEN-FREE • SOY-FREE • NUT-FREE • SUGAR-FREE

Serving cauliflower at a party may sound like an idea that's been played out, but when you put a tangy tikka spin on it, this version will bring back the shine to any veggie tray!

Preheat the oven to 400°F (200°C, or gas mark 6) and line a baking sheet with parchment paper.

In a food processor or blender, purée the yogurt, lemon juice, ginger, garlic, jalapeño, turmeric, cumin, garam masala, sea salt, and pepper together until mostly smooth. In a large bowl, toss the sauce with the cauliflower florets until they are evenly coated and then spread them out over the parchment paper.

Roast the cauliflower for 20 to 25 minutes, flipping the florets halfway through as to not burn one side. Once the cauliflower is roasted and lightly browned, take the baking sheet out of the oven and brush the florets with the melted coconut oil.

Place the cauliflower in a serving bowl, sprinkle the cilantro on top, and serve along with toothpicks or a serving spoon.

YIELD: 4 servings

1 cup (230 g) plain coconut milk yogurt

2 tablespoons (28 ml) lemon juice

1 tablespoon (6 g) minced fresh ginger

2 cloves of garlic, minced

1 tablespoon (6 g) minced fresh jalapeño

1 teaspoon ground turmeric

½ teaspoon ground cumin

½ teaspoon garam masala

½ teaspoon sea salt

Pinch of freshly ground black pepper

2 pounds (910 g) cauliflower, cut into florets

¼ cup (54 g) coconut oil, melted

3 tablespoons (3 g) chopped fresh cilantro

MOZZ-STUFFED NEATBALLS

GLUTEN-FREE OPTION • SUGAR-FREE

Herbed nut meat encapsulates melty vegan mozzarella while resting gently in a pool of aromatic marinara sauce for this tasty appetizer. Fancy, satisfying, and oh-so-delicious, these stuffed neatballs are perfect for dinner parties.

Preheat the oven to 350°F (180°C, or gas mark 4) and line a baking sheet with a silicone baking mat or parchment paper.

In a food processor, pulse the almonds and walnuts until they resemble coarse sand. Transfer the nuts to a large bowl and stir in the chickpea flour, fennel seeds, onion powder, salt, and black pepper.

In another bowl, whisk the hot vegetable broth, liquid aminos, and vegan Worcestershire sauce together. Pour this wet mixture into the dry mixture and stir until thoroughly combined. Let it rest for 10 minutes before kneading the mixture again and dividing it into 12 equal-size pieces.

Place 1 piece of the neatball mixture in the palm of your hand and make a cup with it. It helps to lightly wet your hands before doing this to prevent sticking. Insert a piece of vegan mozzarella and form the neatball around it to cover it completely. Place on the baking sheet and repeat with the remaining 11 pieces. Use cooking spray to lightly coat the neatballs.

Bake for 15 minutes and then flip the neatballs over and lightly coat the other side with cooking spray. Bake for an additional 10 minutes. Warm the Quicky Marinara Sauce in a saucepan, if necessary, while the neatballs are baking.

Divide the marinara sauce among 4 bowls, place 3 neatballs in each bowl, and finish with basil chiffonade. Serve hot.

YIELD: 4 servings

---

1 cup (145 g) raw almonds

1 cup (100 g) walnuts

½ cup (60 g) chickpea flour

1 teaspoon fennel seeds

½ teaspoon onion powder

¼ teaspoon salt

⅛ teaspoon freshly ground black pepper

½ cup (120 ml) vegetable broth, heated (gluten-free, if necessary)

1 tablespoon (15 ml) liquid aminos or tamari

1 tablespoon (15 ml) vegan Worcestershire sauce (gluten-free, if necessary)

5 ounces (140 g) vegan mozzarella, cut into 12 pieces

Cooking oil spray

1 batch of Quicky Marinara Sauce (page 195)

¼ cup (10 g) fresh basil leaves, chiffonade-cut

CRUDITÉ BOUQUETS

GLUTEN-FREE • SUGAR-FREE

Need a healthy and simple snack in a pinch? Make these crudité bouquets, which are essentially your own personal veggie tray. Pair fresh vegetables with a creamy sauce, in small bowls, and you are ready to go!

Divide the Silky Sour Cream or Irresistable Ranch Dressing among eight 4-ounce (120 ml) ramekins. Arrange the vegetables in the ramekins, standing up, like you would a cute flower arrangement. Arrange the chives among the vegetables, like you might do with ferns in a vase. Refrigerate until ready to serve.

YIELD: **8 servings**

1 batch of Silky Sour Cream (page 194), or ½ of a batch Irresistable Ranch Dressing (page 192)

16 strips of yellow bell pepper

12 green beans, ends trimmed and cut in half

8 radishes, tops trimmed

2 stalks of celery, cut into 8 pieces

1 carrot, cut into 8 matchsticks, or 8 baby carrots

40 fresh chives

CURRY-SPICED SWEET POTATO CHIPS

GLUTEN-FREE • NUT-FREE • SUGAR-FREE

Sweet potato chips are delicious in their own right, but by spicing them up with a curry blend and a kick from cayenne pepper and pairing them with a sriracha aioli, these chips turn delightfully addictive.

To make the chips: Preheat the oven to 350°F (180°C, or gas mark 4) and line 2 baking sheets with parchment paper.

Using a mandoline or sharp knife, cut the sweet potatoes into slices about ⅛ inch (3 mm) thick. Place all the slices in a large bowl, drizzle with the olive oil, and toss until they are evenly coated.

Spread the slices out over the baking sheets, making sure that they are not overlapping. In a small bowl, whisk together the curry powder, salt, cinnamon, smoked paprika, and cayenne. Sprinkle half of the mixture over the two baking sheets of sweet potatoes and bake them for 10 minutes.

Take the chips out of the oven, carefully flip them over, sprinkle with the remaining spice mixture, and bake for 10 more minutes or until lightly browned. Place the baking sheets on cooling racks for 10 minutes. When the chips have hardened a bit, transfer them to a serving bowl.

To make the spicy aioli: Stir together the vegan mayonnaise, sriracha, and garlic powder until combined. Serve with the chips.

YIELD: 4 small servings

FOR THE CHIPS:

1 pound (455 g) sweet potatoes, peeled

2 tablespoons (28 ml) olive oil

1 tablespoon (6 g) yellow curry powder

½ teaspoon salt

⅛ teaspoon ground cinnamon

⅛ teaspoon smoked paprika

⅛ teaspoon cayenne pepper

FOR THE SPICY AIOLI:

¼ cup (60 g) vegan mayonnaise

1 tablespoon (15 ml) sriracha hot sauce

¼ teaspoon garlic powder

WALNUT CHORIZO BEAN DiP

GLUTEN-FREE • SUGAR-FREE

Here's another dip inspired by my mother! Seasoned walnut chorizo, beans on beans, and pickled jalapeños make this snack flavorful, protein-rich, and also high in fiber! This way you can enjoy your snack and feel fuller, too.

In a large pot over medium heat, stir together the Walnut Chorizo, pinto beans, refried beans, water, nutritional yeast, pickled jalapeños, and hot sauce. Bring to a simmer, adjust the heat to medium-low, and continue simmering for 15 to 20 minutes.

Season the dip with salt, transfer to a serving bowl, and serve warm with a large bowl of corn chips because it's party time!

YIELD: 8 servings

½ of a batch of Walnut Chorizo (page 73)

1 can (15 ounces, or 425 g) pinto beans

1 can (15.5 ounces, or 435 g) vegan refried beans

1 cup (235 ml) water

5 tablespoons (19 g) nutritional yeast

2 tablespoons (18 g) minced pickled jalapeños

1 tablespoon (15 ml) hot sauce of your choice

Pinch of salt

Corn chips, for serving

ROASTED BROCCOLINI AMANDINE

GLUTEN-FREE • SOY-FREE • SUGAR-FREE

You really can't go wrong with roasting broccolini. It's sweeter than broccoli and it tastes excellent when paired up with garlic and toasted almonds.

Preheat the oven to 375°F (190°C, or gas mark 5) and line a baking sheet with parchment paper.

In a large bowl, toss together the broccolini, olive oil, garlic, and oregano and then spread the mixture out on the baking sheet in a single layer.

Bake for 10 minutes and then take the baking sheet out of the oven and sprinkle the almond slices, salt, and pepper over the top. Return to the oven and bake for 5 more minutes to brown the almonds slightly. Serve hot.

YIELD: 4 small servings

¾ pound (340 g) broccolini

2 tablespoons (28 ml) olive oil

3 cloves of garlic, thinly sliced

¼ teaspoon dried oregano

⅓ cup (32 g) sliced almonds

¼ teaspoon salt

Pinch of freshly ground black pepper

CRISPY PORTOBELLO STRIPS

GLUTEN-FREE • SOY-FREE • NUT-FREE OPTION

Fried zucchini is cool, but have you ever had fried portobello mushroom strips? This is a whole other tier of crispy veggie that everyone must try! Plus, anything dipped in ranch dressing is pretty much guaranteed to be tasty.

Heat 1 inch (2.5 cm) of mild-flavored cooking oil in a cast-iron skillet over medium heat to 375°F (190°C).

Slice the portobello mushrooms into ½-inch (1.2 cm)-wide strips. Dust the strips with the 1 tablespoon (7 g) chickpea flour.

In a large bowl, whisk together the remaining ¼ cup (30 g) chickpea flour, cornmeal, panko bread crumbs, onion powder, salt, thyme, and black pepper. Stir in the soy-free nondairy milk until combined, with no dry pockets.

Carefully dunk a few of the portobello strips into the breading mixture, coating them fully but letting the excess drip off. Place in the hot oil, being careful not to overcrowd the pan, and fry for 4 minutes. Flip and fry for an additional 3 minutes or until golden brown.

Remove the mushrooms with a slotted spoon and lay them on a paper towel–lined plate to drain. Repeat the dunking and frying process until all the mushroom strips have been fried. Serve hot with Quicky Marinara Sauce and/or Irresistible Ranch Dressing.

YIELD: 4 small servings

Mild-flavored cooking oil, for frying

½ pound (225 g) portobello mushrooms

¼ cup (30 g) plus 1 tablespoon (8 g) chickpea flour

⅓ cup (47 g) cornmeal

¼ cup (40 g) gluten-free panko bread crumbs

½ teaspoon onion powder

½ teaspoon salt

¼ teaspoon dried thyme

Pinch of freshly ground black pepper

1 cup (235 ml) unsweetened soy-free nondairy milk (nut-free, if necessary)

Quicky Marinara Sauce (page 195) and/or Irresistible Ranch Dressing (page 192), for dipping (forgo the ranch dressing if nut-free is necessary)

BAKED ONION RINGS WITH BARBECUE AND SMOKY TAHINI SAUCES

SOY-FREE • NUT-FREE

Pair these crispy baked onion rings slathered in smoky sweet sauces with your favorite beer and be transported to Happy Hour Heaven at home.

Preheat the oven to 375°F (190°C, or gas mark 5) and line a large baking sheet with parchment paper.

Place ¼ cup (31 g) of the flour in one shallow dish and then whisk the remaining ¾ cup (94 g) flour, cornmeal, salt, parsley, and garlic powder together in another shallow dish. Pour the soy-free nondairy milk into a third shallow dish.

Separate the onion slices into individual rings and coat them first in just the flour, then dip them into the nondairy milk, and then coat the rings in the cornmeal-flour mixture. Set each ring on the baking sheet.

Spray a light coating of cooking oil spray over the rings and bake for 12 minutes. Flip each ring over, spray another light coat of cooking oil spray over them, and bake for an additional 12 to 15 minutes until the edges start to brown.

Place the onion rings in a serving bowl and drizzle Strawberry Barbecue Sauce and Smoky Tahini Sauce over the top, or if you prefer, leave the sauces on the side for dipping. Sprinkle the parsley over the rings and serve hot.

YIELD: 4 small servings

1 cup (125 g) unbleached all-purpose flour, divided

¼ cup (35 g) cornmeal

1 teaspoon salt

½ teaspoon dried parsley

¼ teaspoon garlic powder

1 cup (235 ml) unsweetened soy-free, nut-free nondairy milk

1 pound (455 g) white onions, sliced ½ inch (1 cm) thick

Cooking oil spray (I use organic canola oil spray.)

¼ cup (65 g) Strawberry Barbecue Sauce (page 193) or vegan barbecue sauce

¼ cup (60 g) Smoky Tahini Sauce (page 199)

1 tablespoon (4 g) minced fresh parsley

GRILLED MANGO WITH RASPBERRY COULIS

GLUTEN-FREE • SOY-FREE • NUT-FREE

Need a healthy snack that is packed with great flavors from grilled mango, sweet raspberries, and tart orange juice? I've got the perfect dish for you.

Prepare a hot fire in a grill (375°F, or 190°C) and oil the grill grates.

While the grill is heating, place the raspberries, orange juice, water, sugar, orange zest, and salt in a blender and purée until smooth. Strain the mixture through a fine-mesh sieve to remove the raspberry seeds. Simmer the coulis in a small saucepan over medium-low heat for 5 to 7 minutes, stirring occasionally.

Grill the mango slices for 2 to 3 minutes on each side until there are dark grill marks.

Toss the mango in a large bowl with the raspberry coulis and serve.

YIELD: 4 servings

6 ounces (170 g) fresh raspberries

¼ cup (60 ml) orange juice

2 tablespoons (28 ml) water

2 tablespoons (28 ml) organic cane sugar

½ teaspoon grated orange zest

Pinch of salt

3 pounds (1.4 kg) mango, seeded, peeled, and sliced into ¼-inch-wide (6 mm) strips

> **Experiment with this recipe by trying it out with some of your favorite fruits. Pineapple, peaches, and plantains are all great for grilling.**

HERBED TOFU TOMATO SALAD

GLUTEN-FREE • NUT-FREE • SUGAR-FREE

Pair the salty, herbed tofu cheese with ripe tomatoes, peppery baby arugula, and a squeeze of fresh lemon, and you have yourself a simple, seasonal salad that doubles as a great side dish.

Wrap the block of tofu tightly in a clean kitchen towel. Place it on a plate and stack some heavy (but stable) objects on it to press the moisture out.
Let it press for 20 to 30 minutes.

In a resealable container or large zip-top plastic bag, whisk together the water, sea salt, coconut vinegar, olive oil, basil, and oregano.

Unwrap the pressed tofu, pat dry, cut it into ½-inch (1.3 cm) cubes, and place it in the marinade. Marinate it for 4 to 8 hours in the refrigerator, depending on how salty you would like it to be. Stir it around or flip the container over every couple of hours. Once the tofu is done marinating, drain it of the excess liquid and toss it together in a large bowl with the tomatoes and arugula.

Drizzle the lemon juice over the top of the salad and sprinkle on the pepper. Chill for 30 minutes and then sprinkle with sea salt, if using, and serve.

YIELD: 4 servings

1 block (12 ounces, or 340 g) extra-firm tofu, rinsed and drained

½ cup (115 ml) water

1½ to 2 tablespoons (23 to 30 g) sea salt

2½ tablespoons (38 ml) coconut vinegar

2 tablespoons (28 ml) olive oil

1 teaspoon dried basil

1 teaspoon dried oregano

4 cups (720 g) chopped tomatoes

3 cups (60 g) packed baby arugula

1 tablespoon (15 ml) lemon juice

Pinch of freshly ground black pepper

Pinch of coarse sea salt (optional)

> If you don't have coconut vinegar, you should really get your hands on some! But if you can't find it, try replacing it with 1 tablespoon (15 ml) apple cider vinegar mixed with 1 tablespoon (16 g) white miso paste.

ROASTED PUMPKIN QUINOA SALAD

GLUTEN-FREE • SOY-FREE • NUT-FREE

Subtly sweet roasted pumpkin, fluffy red quinoa, and beautiful rainbow chard come together with a tangy dressing to create a wholesome autumnal salad that is delicious and satiating.

Preheat the oven to 375°F (190°C, or gas mark 5) and line a baking sheet with parchment paper.

In a large bowl, toss the cubed pumpkin, sunflower oil, and salt together until evenly coated. Spread the pumpkin over the baking sheet and roast for 15 minutes. Flip the pumpkin pieces over, using a spoon, and roast for an additional 10 minutes.

While the pumpkin is roasting, place the quinoa and water in a large saucepan over medium-low heat and cover with the lid. Bring to a simmer and cook for 20 minutes or until the liquid is absorbed. Remove from the heat and fluff with a fork.

Whisk the vegan honey, apple cider vinegar, olive oil, red pepper flakes, and salt together until well combined. In a large bowl, toss the roasted pumpkin, quinoa, chard, and vinaigrette together. Serve immediately or chill in the refrigerator for 45 to 60 minutes before serving.

YIELD: 4 servings

2 pounds (910 g) pumpkin, peeled and cubed

1 tablespoon (15 ml) sunflower oil

⅛ teaspoon salt

1 cup (188 g) red quinoa

2 cups (475 ml) water

¼ cup (80 g) vegan honey (such as Bee Free Honee) or (60 ml) agave nectar

3 tablespoons (45 ml) apple cider vinegar

2 tablespoons (28 ml) olive oil

½ teaspoon crushed red pepper flakes

¼ teaspoon salt

½ pound (225 g) rainbow chard, chopped

ASPARAGUS RIBBON SALAD

GLUTEN-FREE • SOY-FREE • NUT-FREE • SUGAR-FREE

Spring has so many gems to offer in terms of seasonal produce! Here we combine ribbons of asparagus with crisp, refreshing shaved fennel, creamy fava beans, and a sweet raisin vinaigrette to create a beautifully bright salad.

In a small pot, bring the water to a boil. Add the fava beans and cook for 4 minutes. Drain the beans and submerge them into a bowl of ice water for 2 minutes. Drain again, pop them out of their skins, and place in a small bowl.

Using a potato peeler, mandoline, or very sharp knife, cut the asparagus, zucchini, and fennel bulb into thin ribbons. Place them in a large bowl and add the sunflower sprouts.

Drain the raisins, reserving ¼ cup (60 ml) of the soaking water. Place the raisins, raisin soaking water, balsamic vinegar, olive oil, salt, and pepper in a blender and purée until smooth.

Toss the vinaigrette with the asparagus, zucchini, fennel, and sprouts. Top with the red grapes and sunflower seeds and serve.

YIELD: 4 servings

2 cups (475 ml) water

1 cup (150 g) fresh fava beans

6 ounces (170 g) asparagus

6 ounces (170 g) zucchini

6 ounces (170 g) fennel bulb

3 ounces (85 g) sunflower sprouts

⅓ cup (50 g) raisins, soaked in hot water to cover

3 tablespoons (45 ml) balsamic vinegar

1 tablespoon (15 ml) olive oil

⅛ teaspoon salt

⅛ teaspoon freshly ground black pepper

1 cup (150 g) halved red grapes

¼ cup (36 g) roasted sunflower seeds

WALNUT CHORIZO TACO SALAD

SOY-FREE OPTION • SUGAR-FREE

When I was a kid, I remember my mom always ordering taco salads whenever we went out to eat at a Mexican restaurant. My baked tortilla shell is a healthier version of the typically deep-fried one, but with this flavorful walnut chorizo filling, I know you won't be missing a thing.

(continued on next page)

(continued from previous page)

To make the walnut chorizo: In a food processor, pulse the walnuts until they turn into small grains, like a coarse sand. Add the apple cider vinegar, chili powder, garlic powder, cumin, coriander, salt, oregano, thyme, pepper, cinnamon, garlic, and bay leaves to the processor and pulse until combined.

Transfer the walnut mixture to a large skillet over medium heat. Brown the chorizo for 10 minutes, stirring occasionally, and then adjust the heat to low and cover with a lid to keep warm.

To make the salad: Preheat the oven to 350°F (180°C, or gas mark 4). Place the tortillas into 4 large ovenproof bowls, creating some pleats so that they can sit flush with the bottom. Put a small ovenproof bowl inside of the tortilla to help hold its shape and then bake the shells for 10 minutes. Remove the inner bowl and bake for 2 more minutes. Let the tortilla shells cool in the bowls for 5 minutes.

Divide the lettuce among the shells. Toss the black beans with the cumin and salt in a bowl and divide the beans among the salads. Top with the walnut chorizo, tomato, onion, and black olives.

Spoon a dollop of Silky Sour Cream, Simple Guacamole, and Roasted Chipotle Salsa onto each salad, finish them with a sprinkle of minced cilantro, and serve.

Note: To make this recipe soy-free, omit the Silky Sour Cream.

YIELD: 4 servings

FOR THE WALNUT CHORIZO:

1 pound (455 g) walnuts

3 tablespoons (45 ml) apple cider vinegar

2 tablespoons (15 g) ground ancho chili powder

1 tablespoon (9 g) garlic powder

1 teaspoon ground cumin

1 teaspoon ground coriander

1 teaspoon salt

½ teaspoon dried oregano

½ teaspoon dried thyme

½ teaspoon freshly ground black pepper

⅛ teaspoon ground cinnamon

⅛ teaspoon ground cloves

2 bay leaves

FOR THE SALAD:

4 large flour tortillas

1 pound (455 g) green leaf lettuce, chopped

1 can (15 ounces, or 425 g) black beans, rinsed and drained

¼ teaspoon ground cumin

⅛ teaspoon salt

1 cup (180 g) chopped tomato

½ cup (80 g) diced red onion

¼ cup (35 g) sliced black olives

¼ cup (60 g) Silky Sour Cream (page 194)

1 batch of Simple Guacamole (optional; page 198)

½ cup (130 g) Roasted Chipotle Salsa (optional; page 46)

2 tablespoons (2 g) minced fresh cilantro

SUMMERY STONE FRUIT SALAD

GLUTEN-FREE • SOY-FREE • NUT-FREE

- -

This fruity salad is simple but exquisite—so many beautiful slices of peaches, plums, nectarines, and cherries, speckled with bright green from the spinach and tingling mint. Up your fruit salad game at the next summer gathering with this stunner!

- -

To make the stone fruit salad: Toss the peaches, plums, nectarines, cherries, spinach, and mint together in a large bowl. Place them in the refrigerator to chill.

To make the mint simple syrup: Place the mint leaves in a glass measuring cup along with the agave nectar and muddle until the leaves have broken down. Whisk the lemon juice and salt into the mixture and strain it through a fine-mesh sieve over the fruit salad. Toss to coat everything evenly and serve.

YIELD: 4 servings

FOR THE STONE FRUIT SALAD:

1 pound (455 g) white peaches, pitted and sliced

¾ pound (340 g) plums, pitted and sliced

6 ounces (170 g) nectarines, pitted and sliced

6 ounces (170 g) sweet dark cherries, pitted and halved

2 cups (60 g) packed ribbon-cut spinach

2 tablespoons (12 g) minced fresh mint

FOR THE MINT SIMPLE SYRUP:

¼ cup (24 g) fresh mint leaves

2 tablespoons (28 ml) agave nectar

2 tablespoons (28 ml) lemon juice

Pinch of salt

GRILLED ROMAINE CHOP SALAD

GLUTEN-FREE • SUGAR-FREE • NUT-FREE

If you have never tried grilling greens before, you are missing out on one of my favorite ways to prepare them. This technique works really well with water-heavy greens like romaine, green leaf, and iceberg lettuces. Add smoky grilled eggplant and fresh veggies to the mix and you get a flavor explosion.

To make the salad: Lay the eggplant out on a plate and sprinkle each side with a light dusting of salt to release some of its juices. After 20 minutes, brush off as much salt as you can, pat the eggplant dry, and put the eggplant slices in a large zip-top plastic bag along with the olive oil, liquid aminos, and liquid smoke. Seal the bag, shake it up, and put it in the refrigerator to marinate for 30 minutes.

Prepare a medium-hot fire in a grill (350°F, or 180°C) and oil the grill grates.

Take the eggplant out of the marinade and set the marinade aside. Place the eggplant on the grill along with the romaine, mushrooms, and corn and cook for 3 to 5 minutes or until there are bold grill marks. Flip everything over and grill for an additional 3 to 5 minutes. Brush some of the leftover marinade over the eggplant for the last half of the grilling time.

Chop the romaine and eggplant into bite-size pieces. Cut the corn kernels off of the cob. Divide the romaine between 2 bowls and top each bowl with eggplant, corn, mushrooms, tomatoes, and cucumber.

To make the dressing: Whisk all of the ingredients together until smooth. Drizzle over the top of each salad and serve.

YIELD: 2 servings

FOR THE SALAD:

½ pound (225 g) eggplant, peeled and cut into ½-inch-thick (1.3 cm) rounds

2 teaspoons salt

2 tablespoons (28 ml) olive oil

1 tablespoon (15 ml) liquid aminos

1 teaspoon gluten-free liquid smoke

1 head of romaine lettuce (1 pound, or 455 g), quartered lengthwise

¼ pound (115 g) cremini mushrooms, stems removed

1 ear of corn, husk removed

1 cup (150 g) grape or cherry tomatoes, cut in half

1 cup (134 g) partially peeled and chopped cucumber

FOR THE DRESSING:

2 tablespoons (28 ml) lemon juice

2 tablespoons (28 ml) olive oil

1½ teaspoons nutritional yeast

½ teaspoon Dijon mustard

¼ teaspoon agave nectar

⅛ teaspoon garlic powder

⅛ teaspoon salt

Pinch of freshly ground black pepper

MIGHTY MANGO PINEAPPLE SALAD

GLUTEN-FREE • SOY-FREE

If you have ever sat at your desk at lunchtime, needing to be swept away to the tropical island of your (day) dreams, this salad would be the one to do it. A dish filled with juicy tropical fruits and coconutty cashews is certainly a memorable one.

To make the salad: In a large bowl, toss the pineapple, mango, papaya, plantain, and cilantro until combined. Place in the refrigerator to chill while you prep the cashews.

To make the cashews: Preheat the oven to 300°F (150°C, or gas mark 2) and line a small baking sheet with parchment paper.

In a small bowl, toss the cashews and agave together until evenly coated. Add the coconut and salt to the bowl and stir gently. Spread the cashews out over the small baking sheet.

Bake for 5 minutes, stir them around to flip, and bake for another 5 minutes. Let cool for a few minutes. Top the fruit salad with the cashews and serve.

YIELD: **4 servings**

FOR THE SALAD:

2 cups (310 g) peeled and chopped pineapple

1 cup (175 g) peeled, seeded, and chopped mango

1 cup (175 g) peeled, seeded, and chopped papaya

1 cup (150 g) peeled and diced very ripe plantain

1 tablespoon (1 g) minced fresh cilantro

FOR THE CASHEWS:

½ cup (70 g) raw cashews

1 tablespoon (15 ml) agave nectar

2 tablespoons (10 g) unsweetened shredded coconut

Pinch of salt

BANH MI PANZANELLA SALAD

GLUTEN-FREE OPTION • NUT-FREE

One of my favorite dishes from a local chain vegan restaurant is the banh mi salad. They took all of what makes a banh mi sandwich great and put it in a bowl! Now I have created an even better version for you and added the bread back in to make it a fun panzanella-style recipe.

To make the quick-pickled veggies: In a tall canning jar, stir the hot water, apple cider vinegar, and sugar together until the sugar has dissolved. Add the carrot, daikon, and cucumber to the jar, shake, and let marinate in the refrigerator for at least 30 minutes.

To make the oyster mushrooms: Preheat the oven to 350°F (180°C, or gas mark 4) and line a baking sheet with parchment paper.

Place the milk in a shallow dish. Sift the rice flour and salt together in another shallow dish.

Dip the mushroom pieces into the nondairy milk, letting any excess drip off, and then coat them in the rice flour. Place the crusted pieces on the baking sheet. Lightly spray both sides of the mushrooms with cooking oil spray and bake for 15 minutes. Flip the pieces over and bake for an additional 10 minutes.

(continued on next page)

FOR THE QUICK-PICKLED VEGGIES:

1 cup (235 ml) hot water

6 tablespoons (90 ml) apple cider vinegar

1½ tablespoons (18 g) organic cane sugar

1 cup (130 g) julienned carrot

1 cup (88 g) julienned daikon radish

1 cup (135 g) julienned cucumber

FOR THE OYSTER MUSHROOMS:

⅓ cup (80 ml) unsweetened nut-free nondairy milk

½ cup (80 g) brown rice flour

½ teaspoon salt

6 ounces (170 g) oyster mushrooms, broken into bite-size pieces

Cooking oil spray

> Though regular basil is great here, if you can get your hands on Thai basil at an Asian or farmers' market, give that a try. Used in traditional banh mi sandwiches, it has a unique flavor.

(continued from previous page)

To make the salad: In a very large bowl, toss the kale, napa cabbage, basil, cilantro, mint, and bread cubes together. Divide the mixture among 4 serving bowls and divide the pickled vegetables among them. Next, divide the oyster mushrooms among the salads.

To make the dressing: Whisk the rice vinegar, hoisin, and water together. Drizzle it over the tops of the salads and serve.

YIELD: 4 servings

FOR THE SALAD:

2 cups (134 g) chopped kale, without stems

2 cups (150 g) shredded napa cabbage

¼ cup (10 g) chopped fresh basil

¼ cup (4 g) chopped fresh cilantro

¼ cup (24 g) chopped mint, without stems

1 French baguette (4 ounces, or 115 g), cubed and lightly toasted (gluten-free, if necessary)

FOR THE DRESSING:

⅓ cup (80 ml) rice vinegar

¼ cup (63 g) vegan hoisin sauce (gluten-free, if necessary)

2 tablespoons (28 ml) water

AUTUMN SALAD WITH CITRUS VINAIGRETTE

GLUTEN-FREE • SOY-FREE

Combining fruits with greens is a great way to liven up any salad, but adding farro for a savory, nutty flavor as well as maple-glazed pecans will give this beautiful dish priority on any holiday table.

To make the glazed pecans: Place all of the ingredients in a small saucepan over medium heat. Bring to a simmer and cook, stirring frequently, until most of the liquid has evaporated and the pecans are coated with the maple mixture. Transfer the pecans to a piece of parchment paper set on a cooling rack.

To make the salad: In a small pot over medium heat, bring the farro and water to a boil. Adjust the heat to medium-low, partially cover the pot with a lid, and cook for 20 to 25 minutes until the water is absorbed and the grains are cooked.

In a large serving bowl, toss the farro and mesclun mix. Arrange the apple and pear slices on top of the salad in a circular fashion and then top with the dried cranberries and glazed pecans.

To make the vinaigrette: Whisk together all of the ingredients until emulsified. Serve the vinaigrette on the side.

YIELD: 4 servings

FOR THE GLAZED PECANS:

½ cup (55 g) pecans

1 tablespoon (15 ml) water

1 tablespoon (15 ml) maple syrup

½ teaspoon ground cinnamon

½ teaspoon vanilla extract

Pinch of salt

FOR THE SALAD:

½ cup (104 g) farro

1 cup (235 ml) water

5 ounces (140 g) mesclun greens

1 apple of your choice, cored and thinly sliced

1 Bosc pear, cored and thinly sliced

¼ cup (30 g) unsweetened dried cranberries

FOR THE VINAIGRETTE:

¼ cup (60 ml) orange juice

3 tablespoons (45 ml) olive oil

1 tablespoon (15 ml) apple cider vinegar

1 tablespoon (15 ml) agave nectar

½ teaspoon grated orange zest

⅛ teaspoon ground ginger

Pinch of ground cinnamon

Pinch of salt

CORN SALAD WITH BASIL PESTO AIOLI

GLUTEN-FREE • SOY-FREE OPTION • NUT-FREE • SUGAR-FREE

This super-tasty side comes together in minutes! Summer corn plus basil pesto aioli is a dreamy combination, not to mention a great way to use up the basil that is oh-so-plentiful in the summer months.

To make the basil pesto aioli: Place the spinach, basil, lemon juice, nutritional yeast, garlic, olive oil, water, salt, and pepper in a food processor and purée until it becomes a paste. Scrape down the sides as necessary. Add the mayo to the processor and pulse until evenly combined.

To make the salad: Toss the corn, spinach, onion, and basil pesto aioli together in a medium bowl. Season with salt and pepper to taste and chill for 15 to 20 minutes before serving.

YIELD: 4 servings

FOR THE BASIL PESTO AIOLI:

2 cups (60 g) packed baby spinach

1 cup (40 g) fresh basil leaves

2 tablespoons (28 ml) lemon juice

1 tablespoon (4 g) nutritional yeast

1 clove of garlic, peeled

1 tablespoon (15 ml) olive oil

1 tablespoon (15 ml) water

½ teaspoon sea salt

¼ teaspoon freshly ground black pepper

½ cup (112 g) vegan mayonnaise (soy-free, if necessary)

FOR THE SALAD:

5 cups (820 g) cooked sweet yellow corn kernels

1 cup (30 g) packed ribbon-cut spinach

⅓ cup (55 g) sliced red onion

Salt and freshly ground black pepper, to taste

WEDGE SALAD WITH PEPITA BACON

GLUTEN-FREE • SOY-FREE

Wedge salads always seemed like such a fancy dish to me when I was younger, most likely because the only time I ever saw them was in restaurants. This is not how it has to be! Make this incredible restaurant-grade wedge salad, topped with crispy shallots, pepita bacon, and creamy ranch dressing at home whenever you like.

To make the pepita bacon: Preheat the oven to 350°F (180°C, or gas mark 4) and line a small baking sheet with aluminum foil.

Toss all of the ingredients together in a small bowl. Spread the mixture out on the baking sheet and roast for 5 minutes. Stir and roast for 3 to 5 more minutes until the seeds are starting to brown.

To make the salad: Heat the olive oil in a small skillet over medium heat. Sauté the shallots for 3 to 5 minutes until they start turning golden brown. Flip the shallots over and cook for another 3 minutes and then transfer them to a paper towel to blot excess oil.

Place 1 wedge of iceberg lettuce into each serving bowl, with the corner side facing upward. Drizzle 2 tablespoons (40 g) of Irresistible Ranch Dressing onto each wedge and then top with the celery, tomatoes, crispy shallots, pepita bacon, and scallions. A crack or two of pepper on top wouldn't hurt either.

YIELD: 4 servings

FOR THE PEPITA BACON:

¼ cup (40 g) raw pumpkin seeds

1 teaspoon maple syrup

½ teaspoon gluten-free liquid smoke

⅛ teaspoon onion powder

⅛ teaspoon garlic powder

⅛ teaspoon salt

FOR THE WEDGE SALAD:

2 tablespoons (28 ml) olive oil

2 shallots, sliced

1 head of iceberg lettuce, cut into quarters

½ cup (120 g) Irresistible Ranch Dressing (page 192)

½ cup (50 g) sliced celery

½ pound (225 g) tomatoes, chopped

2 tablespoons (12 g) diced scallions

Freshly cracked black pepper, to taste (optional)

TEX-MEX POTATO SALAD

GLUTEN-FREE • NUT-FREE • SUGAR-FREE

Cravable, creamy potato salad is spiced up with a pinch of cayenne and studded with black beans, corn, bell pepper, and more in this recipe.

Place the potatoes in a large pot and cover them with water. Bring to a boil over medium-high heat and then adjust the heat to medium and cook for 20 minutes or until fork-tender. Drain the potatoes and transfer them to a bowl.

Add the red onion, celery, black beans, corn, bell pepper, mayo, apple cider vinegar, salt, and cayenne to the bowl and stir until combined. Stir together firmly to smash some of the potatoes slightly for a creamier potato salad.

Refrigerate the potato salad for 1 to 2 hours and serve chilled.

YIELD: 4 to 6 servings

¾ pound (340 g) multicolor fingerling potatoes, chopped

¼ cup (40 g) diced red onion

1 stalk of celery, diced

½ cup (120 g) cooked black beans

½ cup (82 g) cooked sweet yellow corn kernels

½ cup (75 g) diced red bell pepper

½ cup (112 g) vegan mayonnaise

1 tablespoon (15 ml) apple cider vinegar

¼ teaspoon salt

Pinch of cayenne pepper

STRAWBERRY CUCUMBER GAZPACHO

GLUTEN-FREE • SOY-FREE • NUT-FREE • SUGAR-FREE

When you are sitting outside on a hot summer day, gazpacho is one of the most cooling things that you can eat. Strawberries bring a delightfully tart note when combined with water-heavy cucumbers, and here they are rounded out by juicy tomatoes, crisp bell peppers, and fragrant basil.

Place the cucumbers, strawberries, tomatoes, bell pepper, red onion, lemon juice, balsamic vinegar, garlic, salt, and pepper in a large blender. Purée until very smooth. Add the basil leaves and pulse until they have broken down into smaller pieces.

Refrigerate the gazpacho for 1 hour before serving. When ready to serve, divide among 4 bowls and top with a light drizzle of olive oil, the basil chiffonade, and cracked pepper.

YIELD: 4 servings

1 pound (455 g) cucumbers, peeled and chopped

½ pound (225 g) strawberries, stems removed

½ pound (225 g) tomatoes, chopped

1 cup chopped (150 g) yellow bell pepper

½ cup (80 g) chopped red onion

2 tablespoons (28 ml) lemon juice

2 tablespoons (28 ml) balsamic vinegar

1 clove of garlic, peeled

½ teaspoon salt

¼ teaspoon freshly ground black pepper

¼ cup (10 g) fresh basil leaves, plus 2 tablespoons (5 g) chiffonade-cut

Olive oil, for drizzling

Cracked black pepper, for garnish

ROASTED CAULIFLOWER TOMATO SOUP

GLUTEN-FREE • SOY-FREE • NUT-FREE • SUGAR-FREE

This soup is the perfect winter weekday meal! Roasting the cauliflower adds a little more depth of flavor to this severely underrated vegetable, while the chickpeas fill you up and the chard offers its deep green veggie nutrients.

Preheat your oven to 375°F (190°C, or gas mark 5) and line a baking sheet with parchment paper.

Toss the cauliflower florets together with the olive oil, salt, and pepper until evenly coated. Spread out on the baking sheet and roast for 30 minutes. Stir the florets halfway through the cooking time to promote even browning.

While the cauliflower is roasting, warm ¼ cup (60 ml) of the vegetable broth over medium heat in a large pot. Once hot, add the onions to the pot and sauté until translucent, about 3 to 5 minutes. Next, add the remainder of the vegetable broth, the tomato sauce, diced tomatoes, and chickpeas.

Bring the mixture to a boil and then lower the heat to a simmer. Add the Swiss chard, Italian seasoning, and red pepper flakes to the soup. Carefully add the roasted cauliflower to the soup, stirring it in slowly. Cover the pot with a lid and simmer for 5 minutes longer. Season with salt and black pepper. Serve hot.

YIELD: 4 servings

2 pounds (910 g) cauliflower florets

1½ teaspoons olive oil

¼ teaspoon sea salt

Pinch of freshly ground black pepper

2 cups (475 ml) gluten-free vegetable broth

1 cup (160 g) diced white onion

1 can (14.5 ounces, or 410 g) organic tomato sauce

1 can (14.5 ounces, or 411 g) organic diced tomatoes

1 can (15 ounces, or 425 g) chickpeas, rinsed and drained

2 cups (72 g) loosely packed chopped Swiss chard

1 teaspoon dried Italian seasoning

¼ teaspoon crushed red pepper flakes

Salt and freshly ground black pepper, to taste

> To add more body to this soup, stir in 1 cup (185 g) cooked quinoa along with the roasted cauliflower.

SMOKY CORN CHOWDER BREAD BOWL

NUT-FREE • SUGAR-FREE

Chowders are among the most comforting foods out there, and corn chowders in particular have always had a special place in my heart. I also am a huge fan of carbs, so this is a recipe consisting of smoky, creamy carbs inside a bowl made of toasty carbs. Luckily, for both you and me, this recipe is not made with heavy cream and instead takes advantage of the inherent starchiness of corn to thicken it.

In a large pot over medium heat, heat the sunflower oil. Add the shallots and garlic to the pot and sauté for 2 to 3 minutes. Add the corn kernels, nutritional yeast, liquid aminos, liquid smoke, smoked paprika, and onion powder to the pot and stir until combined.

Add the vegetable broth and nondairy milk to the corn mixture and bring to a boil. Reduce the heat to medium-low and carefully use an immersion blender to purée about half of the corn kernels (so it remains slightly chunky).

Cover the pot, bring the soup to a simmer, and cook for 10 minutes, stirring occasionally. Fold the spinach and basil into the soup and cook for another 5 minutes. Meanwhile, preheat the oven to 300°F (150°C, or gas mark 2). Cut the tops out of the bread bowl loaves and cut the bread out of the center, leaving a roughly 1 inch (2.5 cm)-thick wall on all sides. Toast the loaves until lightly golden.

Season the soup with salt and pepper to taste and divide it among the bread bowls. Garnish with a sprinkle of smoked paprika and chiffonade-cut basil and serve immediately.

YIELD: 4 servings

1 teaspoon sunflower oil

2 shallots, diced

1 clove of garlic, minced

4 cups (616 g) fresh corn kernels (or thawed frozen corn)

¼ cup (15 g) nutritional yeast

1 tablespoon (15 ml) liquid aminos

1 teaspoon liquid smoke

¾ teaspoon smoked paprika, plus more for garnish

½ teaspoon onion powder

1½ cups (355 ml) vegetable broth

1 cup (235 ml) unsweetened, nut-free nondairy milk

2 cups (60 g) packed baby spinach

2 tablespoons (5 g) chiffonade-cut fresh basil, plus more for garnish

4 sourdough bread bowls (8 ounces, or 225 g, each)

½ teaspoon salt, or to taste

Freshly ground black pepper, to taste

If you do not have an immersion blender, you can transfer half of the soup to a blender in small batches and carefully purée it with a towel over the top instead of the lid (or else you run the risk of it exploding everywhere).

TEMPEH STOUT CHILI

GLUTEN-FREE OPTION • NUT-FREE • SUGAR-FREE

I was lucky enough recently to be invited to participate in a Vegan Chili Cook-Off, put on by Tony's Darts Away in Burbank, California. I made a slightly different version of this chili for the competition, and it got rave reviews! The key here is the cool avocado crema, crunchy cheddar crisps, and bold chili all complementing each other in the best way possible.

To make the avocado crema: Place all of the ingredients in a blender and purée until very smooth. Taste and adjust the salt as desired and refrigerate the crema while preparing the chili.

To make the cheddar crisps: Preheat the oven to 350°F (180°C, or gas mark 4) and line a baking sheet with a silicone baking mat or parchment paper.

Spread the cheddar shreds over the baking sheet, making sure that they in a thin layer. Bake for 10 minutes. Let cool on a cooling rack for 15 to 20 minutes until hardened. Break the large crisp into smaller, bite-size pieces.

To make the chili: Steam the tempeh for 15 minutes so that it loses some of its bitterness and then let cool a bit. In a large pot, heat the oil over medium heat. Add the onion and bell pepper and break the tempeh into crumbles into the pan. Sauté until the onions become translucent.

Adjust the heat to medium-low and stir in the black beans, nutritional yeast, chili powder, cumin, ground chipotle chile powder, smoked paprika, bay leaf, and tomato paste. Cook for 5 minutes, stirring frequently, and then add the diced roasted tomatoes, beer, and tomato sauce. Cover with a lid, bring to a simmer, and cook for 15 minutes, stirring occasionally.

Remove the bay leaf, stir in the salt and pepper, and divide the chili among 4 bowls. Drizzle the avocado crema over the chili and top each serving with a few cheese crisps.

YIELD: 4 servings

FOR THE AVOCADO CREMA:

¼ pound (115 g) tomatillos, husked and chopped

½ cup (115 g) mashed avocado

¼ cup (4 g) fresh cilantro leaves

2 tablespoons (28 ml) each lime juice and water

Salt, to taste

FOR THE CHEDDAR CRISPS:

¼ cup (28 g) vegan cheddar shreds (I use Daiya.)

FOR THE CHILI:

8 ounces (225 g) tempeh (gluten-free, if necessary)

1 tablespoon (15 ml) sunflower oil

1 cup (160 g) diced white onion

½ cup (75 g) diced yellow bell pepper

1 cup (240 g) cooked black beans

1 tablespoon (4 g) nutritional yeast

2½ teaspoons (6.5 g) chili powder

1½ teaspoons ground cumin

¼ teaspoon each ground chipotle chile powder and smoked paprika

1 bay leaf

1 tablespoon (16 g) tomato paste

1 can (14.5 ounces, or 410 g) diced roasted tomatoes

1 cup (235 ml) stout beer (or gluten-free beer, if necessary)

½ cup (123 g) tomato sauce

1 teaspoon salt

Freshly ground black pepper, to taste

KABOCHA SQUASH POZOLE

GLUTEN-FREE • SOY-FREE • NUT-FREE

Did you know that pozole was once a dish made with meat from humans that had been sacrificed to the gods by the Aztecs? Thankfully, we do not have to worry about anything like that now, and we can focus on the wonderful flavors of kabocha squash, Hatch chiles, and hominy!

To make the pozole: In a large pot over medium heat, heat the olive oil. Add the kabocha squash and Hatch chiles to the pot and brown them for 7 to 9 minutes, stirring occasionally so that the squash does not stick to the pot.

Stir the garlic, chili powder, oregano, and cumin into the pot with the squash and sauté for 2 minutes. Add the vegetable broth, water, and tomato sauce to the pot and bring to a boil. Adjust the heat to medium-low and simmer for 20 minutes or until the squash is fork-tender.

Stir the hominy into the pozole and season with salt. Simmer just long enough to heat the hominy through and then divide among 4 bowls.

To assemble: Top each bowl with cabbage, Roasted Chipotle Salsa, avocado, and lime wedges. Serve immediately.

YIELD: 4 servings

> If you can't get your hands on fresh Hatch chiles, canned diced green chiles, drained, will work in a pinch.

FOR THE POZOLE:

1 tablespoon (15 ml) olive oil

2 pounds (910 g) kabocha squash, peeled and cubed

¼ pound (115 g) Hatch chiles, seeded and diced

2 cloves of garlic, minced

1 tablespoon (8 g) chili powder

1 teaspoon dried oregano

1 teaspoon ground cumin

3 cups (700 ml) gluten-free vegetable broth

2 cups (475 ml) water

1 can (15 ounces, or 425 g) no-salt-added tomato sauce

1 can (25 ounces, or 710 g) hominy, rinsed and drained

1½ teaspoons salt, or to taste

FOR THE ASSEMBLY:

½ cup (35 g) shredded green cabbage

½ cup (130 g) Roasted Chipotle Salsa (page 46)

½ cup (73 g) pitted, peeled, and cubed avocado

8 lime wedges

CHEEZY POTATO SOUP

GLUTEN-FREE • NUT-FREE

I worked in a very not-vegan-friendly restaurant back when I was in college, and it had a hugely popular loaded potato soup on the menu. This recipe is a shout-out to my college self as well as to my family, who love this creamy-without-the-cream version of the soup just as much as the original.

To make the soup: Place the potatoes in a large pot and cover them with water. Bring to a boil over high-medium heat and then adjust the heat to medium and cook for 15 to 20 minutes until fork tender. Drain the potatoes and return them to the pot.

In a small pan, heat the coconut oil over medium heat and then sauté the onion until translucent. Add the onion, vegetable broth, nondairy milk, yogurt, nutritional yeast, tomato paste, and mustard to the potatoes; stir together.

Bring the mixture to a simmer and then adjust the heat to medium-low. Carefully use an immersion blender (see note on page 92) to purée about half of the mixture so that it remains pretty chunky. Simmer for an additional 10 minutes and stir in the salt, black pepper, and cayenne.

To assemble: Divide the soup among 6 bowls and top each one with Tempting Tempeh Bacon, Silky Sour Cream, chives, and cracked pepper. Serve immediately.

YIELD: 6 servings

FOR THE SOUP:

3 pounds (1.4 kg) yellow potatoes, peeled and chopped

1 tablespoon (14 g) coconut oil

1 cup (160 g) diced white onion

2 cups (475 ml) gluten-free vegetable broth

1 cup (235 ml) unsweetened nut-free nondairy milk

½ cup (115 g) plain nondairy yogurt

½ cup (30 g) nutritional yeast

1 tablespoon (16 g) tomato paste

1 tablespoon (15 g) Dijon mustard

1 teaspoon salt

¼ teaspoon freshly ground white pepper

¼ teaspoon cayenne pepper (optional)

FOR THE ASSEMBLY:

½ of a batch of Tempting Tempeh Bacon (page 197)

Silky Sour Cream (page 194), for dolloping

3 tablespoons (9 g) chopped fresh chives

Cracked black pepper, to taste

MUSHROOM WILD RICE SLOW COOKER STEW

NUT-FREE • GLUTEN-FREE • SUGAR-FREE • SOY-FREE

Slow cookers are a highly under-utilized appliance, in my opinion. So to help win over any skeptics, here is a hearty stew of mixed mushrooms, wild rice, filling black lentils, and fresh herbs that will have you set for dinner with putting too much effort into it.

In a small pan, heat the sunflower oil over medium heat. Add the onions and baby bella mushrooms and sauté for 3 to 5 minutes until the onions become translucent and the mushrooms have reduced in size.

Place the onion-mushroom mixture in a 4-quart (3.8 L) slow cooker, along with the dried porcini mushrooms, lentils, rice, sage, thyme, and rosemary. Toss the ingredients together and then cover with the vegetable broth and water. Cover with the lid and cook for 7 to 8 hours on high, stirring occasionally.

Before serving, stir in the salt and pepper and pick out the thyme and rosemary stems if possible.

Garnish each bowl with a sprig or two of rosemary and serve.

Note: Check the label on the wild rice package to make sure it is soy-free.

YIELD: 4 servings

1 tablespoon (15 ml) sunflower oil

1½ cups (240 g) diced white onion

½ pound (225 g) baby bella mushrooms, sliced

1 ounce (28 g) dried porcini mushrooms, chopped

1 cup (192 g) black lentils

1 cup (160 g) wild rice

1 tablespoon (3 g) chopped fresh sage leaves

4 sprigs of fresh thyme

3 sprigs of fresh rosemary, plus more for garnish

7 cups (1.6 L) gluten-free, soy-free vegetable broth

3 cups (710 ml) water

2 teaspoons salt

1 teaspoon freshly ground black pepper

MEAN GREEN RAMEN

NUT-FREE • SUGAR-FREE

For the first part of my adult life, ramen was something that was eaten out of a plastic cup, when you were busy spending all your money on school supplies and beer. (I'm talking college here.) I've been lucky enough to experience traditional ramen since then, and though there are a few different types, here I give you a miso-based broth version loaded up with green veggies.

Heat the sesame oil in a large soup pot over medium heat. Add the ginger and garlic and sauté for 2 minutes. Add the water, vegetable broth, soy sauce, and dulse granules to the pot and bring to a boil.

Add the miso paste and ramen noodles to the boiling water and cook the noodles according to the package instructions. For the last 2 to 3 minutes of the cooking time, add the bok choy, broccoli, tofu, and mushrooms to the pot.

Stir the soup, making sure the miso paste has fully dissolved. Remove from the heat and carefully divide the ramen among 4 large soup bowls. Top each bowl with a few strips of nori, ¼ cup (26 g) mung bean sprouts, and a drizzle of chili-sesame oil, if using. Serve hot.

YIELD: 4 servings

> Dulse is a type of seaweed. Dried granules and flakes can be found at some well-stocked grocery stores or online.

2 teaspoons untoasted sesame oil

2 tablespoons (16 g) grated fresh ginger

6 cloves of garlic, minced

8 cups (1.9 L) water

2 cups (475 ml) vegetable broth

¼ cup (60 ml) soy sauce

1 teaspoon dulse seaweed granules

¼ cup (63 g) yellow miso paste

8 ounces (225 g) ramen noodles (also called chuka soba)

2 heads of baby bok choy, quartered

2 cups (142 g) broccoli florets

1 package (14 ounces, or 390 g) firm tofu, cubed

3½ ounces (100 g) maitake mushrooms, broken into smaller pieces

2 sheets of nori seaweed, cut into strips

1 cup (104 g) mung bean sprouts

Chili-sesame oil, for drizzling (optional)

FRENCH ONION SOUP

Rich and luxurious, French onion soup is one of those dishes that you picture eating either in an elegant French restaurant with a fine red wine or by a fire in a log cabin, surrounded by flannel and knitted things. I much prefer the latter, and offer up this home-style soup to complete the scene.

In a large skillet over medium heat, melt the coconut oil. Add the onions and sprinkle the sugar and salt over the top of them; sauté for 5 minutes. Reduce the heat to medium-low and cook the onions for 30 to 40 minutes, stirring occasionally. You may need to reduce the heat more so that the onions caramelize to a deep golden brown, but do not burn.

For the last 5 to 10 minutes of the onions cooking, warm the broth, Worcestershire sauce, nutritional yeast, thyme, and ginger in a large pot over medium heat. Once the onions are caramelized, sprinkle the flour over them and then add the sherry cooking wine and deglaze the skillet, scraping up any onion bits that have stuck to it. Simmer for 5 minutes and then add the onions to the pot with the broth.

Bring the soup to a boil and then reduce the heat so that it simmers, covered, for 20 minutes. Meanwhile, preheat the broiler.

When the onions are soft and the soup has thickened slightly, divide it among 4 ovenproof soup mugs. Set the mugs on a baking sheet. Slather 2 tablespoons (27 g) of White Bean Beer Fondue on each piece of bread and place a piece on top of each mug. Broil the soup until the fondue starts to brown slightly and serve immediately.

YIELD: 4 servings

3 tablespoons (42 g) coconut oil

1½ pounds (680 g) yellow onions, sliced

2 teaspoons organic cane sugar

1 teaspoon salt

3½ cups (825 ml) vegetable broth

3 tablespoons (45 ml) vegan Worcestershire sauce

3 tablespoons (12 g) nutritional yeast

½ teaspoon dried thyme

⅛ teaspoon ground ginger

1 tablespoon (8 g) all-purpose flour

½ cup (120 ml) sherry cooking wine

½ cup (108 g) White Bean Beer Fondue (page 45)

4 slices (1 inch, or 2.5 cm thick) of crusty sourdough bread

SICK DAY VEGGIE NOODLE SOUP

GLUTEN-FREE OPTION · SOY-FREE · NUT-FREE · SUGAR-FREE

This simple vegetable soup is just what you need when you are feeling under the weather and want to get something warm, delicious, and nurturing into your system. Brussels sprouts, carrots, zucchini, and celeriac (one of my favorite root vegetables) provide nutritious substance to the seasoned broth and noodles.

Heat the olive oil in a large pot over medium heat. Sauté the onion, Brussels sprouts, celeriac, and carrots until the onions are translucent. Add the zucchini to the pot, sauté for 5 more minutes, and then add the vegetable broth and poultry seasoning. Bring the soup to a boil.

Add the angel hair pasta pieces, cover, and cook for 10 minutes or until the noodles are soft. Stir in the salt and pepper and serve.

YIELD: 6 servings

2 teaspoons olive oil

1 cup (160 g) diced white onion

1 pound (455 g) Brussels sprouts, trimmed and thinly sliced lengthwise

½ pound (225 g) celeriac, peeled and diced

¼ pound (115 g) rainbow carrots, sliced into coins

½ pound (225 g) zucchini, quartered lengthwise, then sliced

8 cups (1.9 L) vegetable broth

1½ teaspoons poultry seasoning (gluten-free, if necessary)

4 ounces (115 g) angel hair pasta, broken up into 1-inch (2.5 cm) pieces (gluten-free, if necessary)

1 teaspoon salt, or to taste

¼ teaspoon freshly ground black pepper

SWEET POTATO EGGPLANT CURRY

GLUTEN-FREE • NUT-FREE • SUGAR-FREE

I did not try eating curries until after college, but ever since my first bite I have been hooked. Green, red, yellow: You name it, I love it. Here we have a yellow curry with sweet potatoes, eggplant, tofu, and jasmine rice. There are so many flavors and enticing aromas!

Wrap the tofu tightly in a clean kitchen towel, set on a plate, and place a couple of weights on top of it to press out some of the moisture. In a large pot over medium heat, melt the coconut oil and sauté the red onion, lemongrass, and ginger until the onions are translucent.

Unwrap the tofu and cut into small cubes; add the sweet potatoes and tofu to the pot and sauté for 5 to 7 minutes until the sides of the tofu are golden. Add the eggplant and curry powder to the pot and sauté for 2 minutes. Add the coconut milk and vegetable broth and bring the curry to a boil.

Add the jasmine rice, reduce the heat to medium-low, cover, and cook for 15 to 20 minutes until the water is absorbed and the rice is cooked.

Stir in the lime juice and salt. Divide the curry among 4 bowls and top each one with toasted coconut and lime zest, and serve.

YIELD: 4 servings

1 package (12 ounces, or 340 g) extra-firm tofu, rinsed and drained

1 tablespoon (14 g) coconut oil

1 cup (160 g) chopped red onion

1 tablespoon (6 g) minced lemongrass

1 tablespoon (6 g) minced fresh ginger

1¼ pounds (570 g) sweet potatoes, peeled and chopped

¾ pound (340 g) eggplant, peeled and chopped

3 tablespoons (19 g) yellow curry powder

1 can (13.5 ounces, or 400 ml) full-fat coconut milk

5 cups (1.2 L) gluten-free vegetable broth

½ cup (92 g) jasmine rice

2 tablespoons (28 ml) lime juice

1½ teaspoons salt

¼ cup (15 g) unsweetened coconut flakes, toasted

1 teaspoon lime zest

Chapter 5

ENTICING ENTRÉE BOWLS

BEAUTIFUL MAINS MADE FOR EVERY CRAVING

This chapter is where things get impressive, selection-wise. Do you have a hankering for mac 'n' cheeze? Or maybe you are more of a taco person? Or perhaps you love eating foods inspired by the cuisines of many different countries? Whatever your preference is, I've got you covered!

SOUTHERN COMFORT BOWL

GLUTEN-FREE • SOY-FREE

When I think of comfort food, I think of Southern cuisine. My versions of some of the Southern classics are healthier but still full of flavor, and this is especially true when it comes to my corn bread and collard greens.

To make the corn bread: Preheat the oven to 400°F (200°C, or gas mark 6) and coat the cups of a standard muffin pan with a thin layer of coconut oil.

Whisk the flaxseed and hot water together and set aside for a few minutes to thicken. In a bowl, whisk the cornmeal, gluten-free flour, salt, baking powder, and cayenne. In another bowl, stir together the nondairy milk, corn kernels, melted coconut oil, agave nectar, and flaxseed mixture.

Fold the wet mixture into the dry mixture until there are no dry clumps and then fill each muffin cup three-quarters full. Bake for 15 minutes or until a toothpick inserted in the center of a muffin comes out clean. Let cool for at least 10 minutes before popping the muffins out of the pan.

To make the chickpea cutlets: Preheat the oven to 375°F (190°C, or gas mark 5) and line a baking sheet with parchment paper.

Pulse the chickpeas and onion in a food processor until it is a crumbly mixture, but not a paste. Transfer to a bowl and fold in the nutritional yeast, aquafaba, salt, poultry seasoning, and black pepper until combined. Sift the rice flour and cornmeal into a shallow dish. Form the chickpea mash into 8 cutlets and gently press them into the flour mixture to coat all sides.

Place the cutlets on the baking sheet and coat with a light spray of cooking oil. Bake for 12 minutes and then flip and bake for an additional 10 to 12 minutes. Let cool for 5 minutes before removing the cutlets from the baking sheet. Roast the okra at the same time.

(continued on next page)

FOR THE CORN BREAD:

1 tablespoon (7 g) ground flaxseed

3 tablespoons (45 ml) hot water

½ cup (70 g) cornmeal

½ cup (68 g) gluten-free all-purpose flour

¾ teaspoon salt

½ teaspoon baking powder

Pinch of cayenne pepper

½ cup (120 ml) unsweetened soy-free nondairy milk

½ cup (77 g) sweet corn kernels

3 tablespoons (42 g) refined coconut oil, melted

2 tablespoons (28 ml) agave nectar

FOR THE CHICKPEA CUTLETS:

2 cans (15 ounces, or 425 g each) chickpeas, drained, liquid reserved

½ cup (80 g) diced white onion

¼ cup (15 g) nutritional yeast

2 tablespoons (28 ml) aquafaba (the liquid drained from the can of chickpeas)

2 teaspoons salt

1 teaspoon salt-free poultry seasoning

½ teaspoon freshly ground black pepper

3 tablespoons (30 g) brown rice flour

1 tablespoon (9 g) cornmeal

Cooking oil spray

(continued from previous page)

To make the okra: In a bowl, toss the okra with the oil, salt, and pepper until evenly coated. Spread the okra out on a small baking sheet lined with foil and roast for 15 to 20 minutes or until the edges start to brown.

To make the collard greens: Melt the coconut oil in a sauté pan over medium heat. Add the onions and sauté until they are translucent. Add the collard greens and black-eyed peas to the pan and cook for 2 minutes.

Stir the liquid smoke, apple cider vinegar, maple syrup, salt, and red pepper flakes into the greens and cook until the greens are wilted but not mushy.

To make the chipotle ranch: Whisk the Irresistable Ranch Dressing, liquid smoke, and chipotle chile powder together until combined.

To assemble: Place 2 cutlets and a corn bread muffin in each of the 4 bowls and then divide the collards and okra among the bowls. Drizzle each one with 1 to 2 tablespoons (20 to 40 g) of chipotle ranch and serve.

YIELD: 4 servings

- The liquid drained from a can of chickpeas, called aquafaba, can be used as an egg substitute in vegan cooking because it has emulsifying and leavening properties.
- Okra is abundant in the summertime. If you cannot find it fresh, you may use frozen. Completely thaw it and then pat dry with paper towels before roasting.

FOR THE OKRA:

3 cups (300 g) chopped okra

1 tablespoon (15 ml) sunflower oil

½ teaspoon salt

⅛ teaspoon freshly ground black pepper

FOR THE COLLARD GREENS:

1 tablespoon (14 g) coconut oil

¼ cup (40 g) diced white onion

6 ounces (170 g) collard greens, stems removed and chopped

1 cup (250 g) cooked black-eyed peas

1½ teaspoons gluten-free liquid smoke

1 teaspoon apple cider vinegar

½ teaspoon maple syrup

½ teaspoon salt

Pinch of crushed red pepper flakes

FOR CHIPOTLE RANCH:

½ cup (120 g) Irresistible Ranch Dressing (page 192)

½ teaspoon gluten-free liquid smoke

¼ teaspoon ground chipotle chile powder

CASHEW-CRUSTED TOFU STIR-FRY

GLUTEN-FREE • SUGAR-FREE

Stir-fries and vegetable sautés were just about all I lived on when I first went vegan. Making them is such a simple way to get tons of nutrients and flavor, all in a weeknight mealtime slot.

To make the tofu: Wrap the tofu in a clean kitchen towel. Place it on a plate and stack some heavy (but stable) objects on it for 15 minutes to press the moisture out. In a food processor, pulse the cashews until they resemble coarse sand. Combine the cashews, rice flour, salt, ginger, and garlic powder in a shallow dish.

Slice the tofu into 12 rectangles and melt the coconut oil in a large skillet over medium heat. Firmly press the tofu into the cashew mixture, coating all sides, and gently place each slice in the hot pan. Cook for 3 to 5 minutes on each side until golden brown. Turn the stove off and keep tofu warm in the skillet while you start the stir-fry.

To make the stir-fry: In a large skillet or wok, melt the coconut oil over medium-high heat. Add the ginger, garlic, and scallions and sauté for 1 minute or until fragrant. Place the bok choy, carrot, broccoli, bell pepper, and sugar snap peas in the skillet and sear for 3 minutes.

Stir the veggies around and sear for 3 more minutes. Deglaze the pan with the sherry and liquid aminos and stir-fry until the broccoli is tender, but not soggy.

To serve: Divide the quinoa (if using) and stir-fried veggies among 4 bowls, top each one with 3 pieces of tofu, and serve.

YIELD: **4 servings**

FOR THE TOFU:

1 package (12 ounces, or 340 g) extra-firm tofu, drained

¼ cup (35 g) raw cashews

3 tablespoons (30 g) rice flour

½ teaspoon salt

¼ teaspoon ground ginger

¼ teaspoon garlic powder

1½ tablespoons (21 g) coconut oil

FOR THE STIR-FRY:

1 tablespoon (14 g) coconut oil

1 tablespoon (8 g) grated fresh ginger

2 cloves of garlic, minced

3 scallions, cut into 1-inch (2.5 cm) pieces

1 head of baby bok choy, cut into 8 wedges

1 large carrot, sliced into coins

1 cup (71 g) chopped baby broccoli

1 cup (150 g) sliced orange bell pepper

1 cup (75 g) sugar snap peas

3 tablespoons (45 ml) sherry cooking wine

3 tablespoons (45 ml) liquid aminos or tamari

FOR SERVING:

2 cups (370 g) cooked quinoa (optional)

BUFFALO CHICKPEA MAC 'N' CHEEZE

GLUTEN-FREE OPTION

Creamy mac 'n' cheeze is paired with easy buffalo-roasted chickpeas, crunchy romaine, and a delicious ranch-style sauce! This recipe is a favorite among my readers, and it is quite easy to understand why when you take a look at those components.

To make the buffalo chickpeas: Preheat the oven to 375°F (190°C, or gas mark 5) and line a baking sheet with parchment paper.

Toss the chickpeas with the ¼ cup (60 ml) buffalo sauce until they are evenly coated and spread them out on the baking sheet. Bake for 12 minutes and then carefully roll them around with a spoon to get the other side crispy. Bake for another 12 to 15 minutes and then place them back in the bowl and toss with the remaining 1 to 2 tablespoons (15 to 28 ml) buffalo sauce. Set aside.

To make the mac 'n' cheeze: Cook the pasta according to the instructions on the package and then drain and rinse with cool water. Place the noodles back in the pot and set the heat to medium-low. Add the Cheezy Cheddar Sauce, salt, and vegan butter (if using) to the pot and stir until the pasta is evenly coated. Add more nondairy milk if you'd like a thinner sauce and season with more salt if necessary. Toss the romaine and celery in with the pasta just before serving.

To assemble: Place about ¼ cup (60 g) of the chickpeas on top of each serving and drizzle with a little extra buffalo sauce and a generous amount of the Irresistable Ranch Dressing.

YIELD: 4 servings

FOR THE BUFFALO CHICKPEAS:

1 can (15 ounces, or 425 g) chickpeas, rinsed and drained

¼ cup (60 ml) of your favorite vegan buffalo sauce, plus 1 to 2 tablespoons (15 to 28 ml)

FOR THE MAC 'N' CHEEZE:

2½ cups (233 g) shell or other small pasta (gluten-free, if necessary)

2 cups (430 g) Cheezy Cheddar Sauce (page 194)

Pinch of salt

1 tablespoon (14 g) vegan butter (optional)

Unsweetened nondairy milk, if needed

2 cups (94 g) chopped romaine lettuce

1 stalk of celery, chopped

FOR THE ASSEMBLY:

Vegan buffalo sauce, for drizzling

½ cup (120 g) Irresistible Ranch Dressing (page 192)

If you cannot find vegan buffalo sauce, combine ¼ cup (60 ml) vinegary hot pepper sauce with 1 tablespoon (14 g) vegan butter.

ORANGE CAULIFLOWER SOBA CHOW MEIN BOWL

NUT-FREE

I will admit, I used to love food court Chinese food, with its greasy chow mein, super-sugary sauces, and of course, the cheesy fortune cookies. Making this zesty orange cauliflower bowl is how I satiate my food court cravings these days, while keeping it healthy.

To make the orange cauliflower: Preheat the oven to 400°F (200°C, or gas mark 6) and line a baking sheet with parchment paper or a silicone baking mat.

Roast the cauliflower for 25 minutes, flipping the florets over after 15 minutes.

While the cauliflower is roasting, heat the sesame oil in a sauté pan over medium heat. Add the garlic and ginger and sauté for 2 minutes. Add the orange juice, sugar, rice vinegar, liquid aminos, orange zest, and red pepper flakes. Bring to a boil and then adjust the heat to medium-low, stirring occasionally. Whisk the water and arrowroot together and then add to the orange sauce, whisking until combined. Cook for 2 to 3 more minutes until the sauce has thickened and coats the back of a spoon.

When the cauliflower is out of the oven, put it in the pan with the orange sauce and toss until well coated.

FOR THE ORANGE CAULIFLOWER:

1 large head of cauliflower, cut into florets

1 teaspoon untoasted sesame oil

1 clove of garlic, minced

2 teaspoons grated fresh ginger

1 cup (235 ml) orange juice

2 tablespoons (24 g) organic cane sugar

1½ tablespoons (23 ml) rice vinegar

1 tablespoon (15 ml) liquid aminos or tamari

1 tablespoon (6 g) grated orange zest

Pinch of crushed red pepper flakes

¼ cup (60 ml) water

1 tablespoon (8 g) arrowroot starch

To make the soba chow mein: Cook the soba noodles according to the package instructions. While the noodles are cooking, heat the untoasted sesame oil in a large skillet over medium heat. Add the napa cabbage, broccoli stalks, and carrots to the pan and sear for 3 minutes. Stir and sear again for 3 minutes.

When the noodles are done cooking, drain them and rinse with cool water. Add the noodles to the pan with the vegetables along with the liquid aminos and toasted sesame oil. Stir together and cook for 2 minutes. Divide among 4 bowls. Divide the cauliflower among the bowls, top with a pinch of red pepper flakes, and serve.

YIELD: 4 servings

FOR THE SOBA CHOW MEIN:

6 ounces (170 g) soba noodles

2 teaspoons untoasted sesame oil

3 cups (225 g) shredded napa cabbage

1 cup (71 g) thinly sliced broccoli stalks

2 carrots, thinly sliced

3 tablespoons (45 ml) liquid aminos or tamari

1 tablespoon (15 ml) toasted sesame oil

Pinch of red pepper flakes

If you have broccoli florets to use up after making this bowl, serve them as dippers for White Bean Beer Fondue (page 45).

SPICY SUSHI BOWL

GLUTEN-FREE OPTION • NUT-FREE

Fluffy sushi rice, topped with fresh veggies, sweet mango, creamy avocado, and a homemade spicy sesame mayo make up this easy-to-prepare sushi bowl. The edamame shines like little green gems and brings the protein, while the panko crumbs give it some crunch.

To make the spicy mayonnaise: Place all of the ingredients in a food processor or blender and purée until completely smooth. Transfer the mayo to a jar or large squeeze bottle and store in the refrigerator for up to 3 weeks. (This recipe makes more than you will need for the sushi bowls.)

To make the sushi bowl: Place the sushi rice, water, and rice vinegar in a pot over medium-low heat, partially cover, and bring to a boil. Lower the heat and simmer for 20 to 25 minutes until the rice is soft, but not mushy. Fluff with a wooden spoon.

Divide the nori strips among 4 bowls, crisscrossing them. Divide the cooked rice among the bowls, as well as the cucumber, daikon radish, mango, avocado, and edamame. Combine the panko bread crumbs and sesame seeds in a small bowl and then sprinkle the crunchies over each bowl. Finish each bowl with a drizzle of spicy mayo. Serve immediately.

YIELD: 4 servings

FOR THE SPICY MAYONNAISE:

1 package (12 ounces, or 340 g) soft silken tofu

¼ cup (60 ml) rice vinegar

¼ cup (60 ml) toasted sesame oil

3 tablespoons (45 ml) sriracha hot sauce

¾ teaspoon salt

¼ teaspoon garlic powder

½ teaspoon agave nectar

FOR THE SUSHI BOWL:

1 cup (180 g) sushi rice

2 cups (475 ml) water

1 tablespoon (15 ml) rice vinegar

2 sheets of nori seaweed, cut into strips

4 ounces (115 g) cucumber, julienne-cut

6 ounces (170 g) daikon radish, julienne-cut

6 ounces (170 g) mango, peeled, seeded, and thinly sliced

1 cup (146 g) sliced avocado

1 cup (150 g) edamame, steamed and removed from pods

3 tablespoons (10 g) panko bread crumbs (gluten-free, if necessary), toasted

1 tablespoon (8 g) sesame seeds, toasted

CABBAGE ROLL BOWL

GLUTEN-FREE OPTION • SUGAR-FREE

My father's side of the family is Polish, and I always looked forward to eating traditional Polish dishes made by my grandmother whenever we visited her. Though she may think this vegan bowl version of her *golabki* is a bit lazy, I'd like to think she'd still love the flavors!

Place the lentils and broth in a small pot and bring to a boil over medium-high heat. Adjust the heat to medium-low, cover partially with a lid, and cook for 25 to 30 minutes until the lentils are tender.

While the lentils are cooking, cut off 8 large leaves at the base of the cabbage. Rinse the leaves, place them in a large pot, and add water to cover. Cover the pot, bring to a boil and then adjust the heat to medium-low and steam the cabbage leaves for 10 to 15 minutes until soft and slightly translucent. Remove with tongs and drain on paper towels.

Once the lentils are cooked, drain the excess liquid and put them in a food processor along with the rest of the ingredients (except the cabbage and Quicky Marinara Sauce). Pulse until the mixture reaches a texture like ground meat. Do not pulse too much or it will become mushy and paste-like.

Place the filling mixture in a pan and heat over medium heat, stirring occasionally.

Place 2 cabbage leaves in each bowl. Divide the filling mixture on top of the leaves, top with Quicky Marinara Sauce, and serve immediately.

YIELD: 4 servings

½ cup (192 g) French lentils

1 cup (235 ml) vegetable broth (gluten-free, if necessary)

1 small head of green cabbage

1 cup (100 g) pecans

⅓ cup (27 g) rolled oats (gluten-free, if necessary)

¼ cup (40 g) chopped white onion

2 tablespoons (7 g) chopped dry-pack sun-dried tomatoes

2 tablespoons (28 ml) olive oil

1½ teaspoons vegan Worcestershire sauce (gluten-free, if necessary)

½ teaspoon liquid aminos or tamari

Salt and freshly ground black pepper, to taste

1 batch of Quicky Marinara Sauce (page 195)

BEANY BURGER BOWL

Burgers can be awesome, but burger bowls are even better because you don't have to worry about adding so many toppings that you can't fit the burger into your mouth. Here's a delicious, basic beany burger bowl that has special sauce and quick pickles and can easily be embellished to suit your cravings.

To make the quick pickles: In a small jar, stir the hot water, white vinegar, sugar, dill, and salt together until the sugar has dissolved. Add the cucumber slices to the jar, shake, and store in the refrigerator for at least 30 minutes.

To make the special sauce: In a small bowl, stir the mayo, ketchup, relish, and mustard together until combined. Place in the refrigerator for 30 minutes to chill before serving.

To make the burger patties: Preheat the oven to 350°F (180°C, or gas mark 4) and line baking sheet with parchment paper.

Pulse the kidney beans and walnuts in a food processor until it is a crumbly mixture, but not a paste. Transfer to a bowl and fold the tomato paste, Worcestershire sauce, sesame oil, onion powder, smoked sea salt, and black pepper into the kidney bean mixture until evenly combined. Form 8 burger patties, approximately ¾ inch (2 cm) thick, and place them on the baking sheet. Bake for 15 minutes and then flip them over and bake for an additional 10 minutes or until they begin to brown lightly. Place the baking sheet on a cooling rack for 5 minutes.

To assemble: Place 3 leaves of butter lettuce in each of the bowls and then divide the toasted bread cubes, tomato slices, and white onion among them. Add 2 burger patties to each bowl, top with pickles, and serve immediately with the special sauce.

YIELD: 4 servings

FOR THE QUICK PICKLES:

3 ounces (90 ml) hot water

2 tablespoons (28 ml) white vinegar

1 teaspoon organic cane sugar

½ teaspoon dried dill

¼ teaspoon salt

1 small pickling cucumber, sliced into rounds

FOR THE SPECIAL SAUCE:

¼ cup (60 g) vegan mayo

2 tablespoons (30 g) ketchup

2 tablespoons (30 g) relish

1½ tablespoons (17 g) yellow mustard

FOR THE BURGER PATTIES:

1 can (15 ounces, or 425 g) kidney beans, rinsed and drained

1 cup (100 g) walnuts

1 tablespoon (16 g) tomato paste

1 tablespoon (15 ml) vegan Worcestershire sauce

1 tablespoon (15 ml) toasted sesame oil

1 teaspoon onion powder

1 teaspoon smoked sea salt

¼ teaspoon freshly ground black pepper

FOR THE ASSEMBLY:

12 butter lettuce leaves

2 thick slices of bread, cubed and toasted

1 cup (180 g) sliced tomatoes

½ cup (80 g) thinly sliced white onion

SNACK SHACK CHILI BILLY

GLUTEN-FREE • SUGAR-FREE

When I was a kid, I played in softball leagues that were all hosted at a park near where I lived. In the middle of the park was the Snack Shack, where we would eat after every game. My favorite meal from the shack was the Chili Billy, made up of crunchy corn chips and hot chili, topped with cheese and sour cream. Making this recipe brought me back to those times, and this version is even better.

To make the easy chili: Place the lentils and vegetable broth in a small pot over medium heat and bring to a boil. Adjust the heat to medium-low and boil, partially covered, for 25 minutes or until the lentils are tender; drain any excess liquid.

In a large pot over medium heat, melt the coconut oil. Add the red onion and Hatch chile and sauté until the onions become translucent. Stir in the lentils, tomato paste, chili powder, ground cumin, and paprika and sauté for 2 minutes.

Add the tomatoes, tomato sauce, water, and apple cider vinegar and bring to a boil. Adjust the heat to medium-low and simmer, uncovered, for 10 to 15 minutes, stirring occasionally. Season with the salt.

To assemble: Divide the corn chips among 4 bowls, topping each with the chili, then Cheezy Cheddar Sauce, Silky Sour Cream, and chives. Serve immediately.

YIELD: 4 servings

FOR THE EASY CHILI:

1 cup (192 g) dried green lentils

2 cups (475 ml) gluten-free vegetable broth

1 teaspoon coconut oil

½ cup (80 g) diced red onion

½ cup (75 g) diced Hatch chile pepper (see note on page 96) or green bell pepper for no spice

1½ tablespoons (24 g) tomato paste

1 tablespoon (8 g) chili powder

1 teaspoon ground cumin

½ teaspoon paprika

1 cup (180 g) diced tomatoes

½ cup (123 g) tomato sauce

½ cup (120 ml) water

1 teaspoon apple cider vinegar

¾ teaspoon salt

FOR THE ASSEMBLY:

1 bag (9 ounces, or 250 g) corn chips

1 cup (215 g) Cheezy Cheddar Sauce (page 194) or (112 g) vegan cheddar shreds

Silky Sour Cream (page 194), for dolloping

¼ cup (12 g) chopped fresh chives

MEDITERRANEAN SPAGHETTI SQUASH

GLUTEN-FREE • SOY-FREE • NUT-FREE • SUGAR-FREE

When I first started learning to cook for myself, I remember being so amazed at how you could use spaghetti squash as a replacement for pasta. Combine the ease of its preparation with the Mediterranean flavors of olives, eggplant, and chickpeas for this great weeknight meal.

Preheat the oven to 350°F (180°C, or gas mark 4) and pour ¼ inch (6 mm) water into the bottom of a large baking dish.

Cut the spaghetti squash in half lengthwise and poke a few holes in the rind with a fork. Lay
the squash cut side down in the baking dish and bake for 40 to 45 minutes until fork-tender. Let cool for 10 minutes.

Heat the olive oil in a large sauté pan, with high walls, over medium heat. Sauté the garlic in the oil for 1 minute and then add the eggplant. Brown the eggplant for 2 minutes and then flip it over and brown for an additional 2 minutes.

Scrape the spaghetti squash strands into the pan and add the chickpeas, sun-dried tomatoes, olives, capers, and oregano. Cook for 5 minutes over medium-low heat and then fold in the spinach, salt, and red pepper flakes. Sauté just until the spinach has wilted. Serve hot.

YIELD: 4 servings

3 pounds (1.4 kg) spaghetti squash

1 tablespoon (15 ml) olive oil

2 cloves of garlic, minced

10 ounces (280 g) eggplant, chopped

1 can (15 ounces, or 425 g) chickpeas, rinsed and drained

½ cup (28 g) julienne-cut dry-pack sun-dried tomatoes

½ cup (70 g) Kalamata olives, sliced

2 tablespoons (18 g) capers with brine

1 teaspoon dried oregano

2 cups (60 g) packed baby spinach

1 teaspoon salt

Pinch of crushed red pepper flakes

JACKFRUIT CHILI VERDE

GLUTEN-FREE • SOY-FREE • NUT-FREE • SUGAR-FREE

Here is a meal that is about as "meat and potatoes" as you can get while remaining vegan. Seasoned jackfruit is used in place of meat, while potatoes add body to a spicy tomatillo and chile pepper base.

Prepare a hot fire in a grill (375°F, or 190°C) and oil the grill grates.

In a large pot, heat the olive oil over medium heat. Add the onion and sauté until translucent. Next, add the garlic, jackfruit, oregano, cumin, and coriander, breaking the jackfruit apart with a wooden spoon while browning it. Cook for 6 to 8 minutes until the jackfruit has reduced in size and browned.

Place the Anaheim chiles, tomatillos, Serrano chile, and jalapeño on the grill. Grill until charred on all sides and then place on a plate and cover with a larger plate or a bowl to steam off the skins. Wait 5 minutes before removing the skins, stems, and seeds from the peppers. Put the tomatillos and peppers into a blender, along with the vegetable broth, puréeing until smooth.

Add the chile mixture and the potatoes to the pot and bring to a boil. Adjust the heat to medium-low and simmer, partially covered, for 25 minutes or until the potatoes are fork-tender. Season with the salt and pepper and serve garnished with the cilantro.

YIELD: 4 servings

1 tablespoon (15 ml) olive oil

½ cup (80 g) diced white onion

2 cloves of garlic, minced

1 can (20 ounces, or 560 g) young jackfruit in brine, drained

1 teaspoon dried oregano

1 teaspoon ground cumin

½ teaspoon ground coriander

4 Anaheim chile peppers

½ pound (225 g) tomatillos, husks removed

1 Serrano chile pepper

1 fresh jalapeño

3 cups (700 ml) gluten-free vegetable broth

1½ pounds (680 g) Idaho potatoes, peeled and chopped

2 teaspoons salt, or to taste

⅛ teaspoon freshly ground black pepper, or to taste

1 tablespoon (1 g) fresh cilantro leaves

> To add more protein to this meal, use 8 ounces (225 g) steamed tempeh or pressed and cubed tofu in place of or in addition to the jackfruit; preparing it in the same manner as the jackfruit. Note that the recipe will no longer be soy-free with the addition of tofu or tempeh.

ROASTED ROOT VEGETABLES WITH SMOKY TAHINI SAUCE

NUT-FREE

If you haven't already picked up on it, I am a huge fan of roasted vegetables. Fall and winter vegetables are prime for roasting and even better when paired with a hearty lentil sausage and smoky tahini sauce. Another root vegetable that would be absolutely perfect for this bowl is the beet! I am allergic to them so I cannot eat them, but I wholeheartedly suggest adding 1 cup (225 g) chopped peeled beets to the vegetable mix before roasting.

(continued on next page)

(continued from previous page)

To make the lentil sausages: Preheat the oven to 375°F (190°C, or gas mark 5) and line a baking sheet with parchment paper (also have ready an unlined baking sheet). In a small pot over medium heat, bring the lentils and vegetable broth to a boil. Adjust the heat to medium-low, cover, and cook for 25 to 30 minutes until the lentils are tender.

Drain the remaining liquid (if any) from the lentils and place in a food processor. Pulse until the lentils have broken up slightly, but are not a paste. Transfer the ground lentils to a bowl and combine with the liquid aminos, maple syrup, onion powder, fennel seeds, paprika, and mustard powder.

Stir the vital wheat gluten into the lentils until it starts binding everything together. Transfer the mixture to a large piece of aluminum foil, forming it into a roughly 1½-inch (3.8 cm)-wide tube. Fold the foil over the sausage, tucking it under and pulling it toward to you tighten the wrap around it. Roll the sausage over one full time and then twist the ends of the foil to make the wrap tight and compress the sausage together. Place the sausage roll on the unlined baking sheet and set aside while you prep the vegetables.

To make the roasted root vegetables: In a large bowl, toss the sweet potatoes, turnips, carrots, and red onion in the olive oil, sprinkle with the salt and pepper, and then toss again. Spread the vegetables out on the lined baking sheet. Put the vegetables and the sausage in the oven and roast for 30 minutes, stirring the vegetables and flipping the sausage after 15 minutes.

To make the farro: While the sausage and vegetables are roasting, place the farro, water, and salt in a small pot and bring to a boil over medium heat. Reduce the heat to medium-low, cover, and cook for 20 to 25 minutes until tender.

To assemble: Divide the farro and roasted vegetables among 4 bowls. Unwrap the lentil sausage and cut into ½-inch-wide (1.3 cm) slices. Divide the sausage among the bowls and finish with a drizzle of Smoky Tahini Sauce. Serve hot.

YIELD: 4 servings

FOR THE LENTIL SAUSAGE:

½ cup (96 g) green lentils

1 cup (235 ml) vegetable broth

2 tablespoons (28 ml) liquid aminos or tamari

1 tablespoon (15 ml) maple syrup

1 teaspoon onion powder

¼ teaspoon fennel seeds

¼ teaspoon paprika

¼ teaspoon mustard powder

¼ cup (25 g) vital wheat gluten

FOR THE ROOT VEGETABLES:

½ pound (225 g) sweet potatoes, chopped

½ pound (225 g) turnips, peeled and chopped

½ pound (225 g) carrots, chopped

1 cup (160 g) chopped red onion

1 tablespoon (15 ml) olive oil

½ teaspoon salt

¼ teaspoon freshly ground black pepper

FOR THE FARRO:

1 cup (208 g) farro

2 cups (475 ml) water

½ teaspoon salt

FOR THE ASSEMBLY:

1 batch of Smoky Tahini Sauce (page 199)

UPSIDE-DOWN SHEPHERD'S PIE

GLUTEN-FREE OPTION • SUGAR-FREE

Imagine it's a rainy, cold, dreary day and all you want to do is to cozy up to a warm meal. What will you be making? This upside-down shepherd's pie, of course! Mashed potatoes topped with hearty pot pie filling will satisfy you without the long oven baking time.

To make the mashed potatoes: Place the potatoes and vegetable broth in a large pot, adding water until the potatoes are covered. Bring to a boil over medium heat and then adjust the heat to medium-low, cover, and cook for 15 to 20 minutes until the potatoes are fork-tender.

Drain the potatoes, reserving 1 cup (235 ml) of the broth, and return them to the pot. Add the nondairy milk, coconut oil, and salt, mashing until slightly chunky. Cover to keep warm.

To make the "filling": In a large skillet, melt the coconut oil over medium heat. Sauté the leeks, carrot, and celery in the oil for 5 minutes, stirring occasionally. Next, add the mushrooms, corn, and peas, sautéing for 5 to 7 minutes, until the mushrooms have reduced in size. Stir in the nutritional yeast, chickpea flour, and vegan Worcestershire sauce.

Pour the reserved vegetable broth into the skillet, stirring until evenly combined. Add the thyme and sage and simmer for 10 minutes or until the mixture has thickened and the carrots are tender. Season with the salt and pepper.

Divide the mashed potatoes among 4 bowls, topping each mound with the "filling" and 2 sprigs of fresh thyme. Serve immediately.

YIELD: **4 servings**

FOR THE MASHED POTATOES:

2 pounds (910 g) russet potatoes, peeled and chopped

3 cups (700 ml) vegetable broth

½ cup (120 ml) unsweetened nondairy milk (gluten-free, if necessary)

2 tablespoons (28 g) coconut oil

1 teaspoon salt, or to taste

FOR THE "FILLING":

1 tablespoon (14 g) coconut oil

1½ cups (134 g) sliced leeks

1 large carrot, sliced into coins

1 stalk of celery, chopped

½ pound (225 g) button mushrooms, sliced

½ cup (154 g) corn kernels

½ cup (75 g) peas

1 tablespoon (4 g) nutritional yeast

1 tablespoon (8 g) chickpea flour

1 tablespoon (15 ml) vegan Worcestershire sauce (gluten-free, if necessary)

5 sprigs of fresh thyme, plus more for garnish

¼ teaspoon ground sage

½ teaspoon salt, or to taste

Pinch of freshly ground black pepper

MEZZE FUSION BOWL

GLUTEN-FREE OPTION • NUT-FREE • SUGAR-FREE

Lots of research went into creating the recipes for this book, mostly on the food traditions and dishes of different cultures. When it comes to the mezze platter, or bowl in this case, there are quite a few differences between what the Greeks, Turks, Lebanese, and Iranians feature. I pulled my favorites from all over and brought them together for one delicious, fusion mezze bowl.

To make the tabbouleh: In a small pan, bring the quinoa and water to a boil over medium heat. Adjust the heat to medium-low, cover, and cook for 20 minutes. Once cooked, transfer to a bowl and refrigerate.

In a large bowl, combine the parsley, tomatoes, white onion, olive oil, and lemon juice. Add the quinoa to the bowl and toss, seasoning with the salt and pepper. Return to the refrigerator for 30 minutes.

To make the baba ghanoush: Prepare a hot fire in a grill (375°F, or 190°C) and oil the grill grates. Place the whole eggplant on the grill and char each side until black. Take eggplant off the grill and let cool for a few minutes before handling.

Once cool enough to handle, slice the eggplant skin and scoop the insides into a food processor, along with the tahini, lemon juice, garlic, cumin, and salt. Purée until smooth.

To assemble: Divide the tabbouleh, baba ghanoush, Herbed Tofu Feta, artichoke hearts, olives, and pita chips among 4 bowls and serve.

YIELD: 4 servings

FOR THE TABBOULEH:

¼ cup (43 g) quinoa, rinsed

⅔ cup (160 ml) water

¼ pound (115 g) fresh curly parsley, minced

¾ cup (135 g) diced Roma tomatoes

¼ cup (40 g) diced white onion

2½ tablespoons (40 ml) olive oil

2 tablespoons (28 ml) lemon juice

¼ teaspoon salt

Freshly ground black pepper, to taste

FOR THE BABA GHANOUSH:

¾ pound (340 g) eggplant

2 tablespoons (30 g) tahini

1 tablespoon (15 ml) lemon juice

1 clove of garlic, peeled

½ teaspoon ground cumin

¼ teaspoon salt

FOR THE ASSEMBLY:

½ of a batch of Herbed Tofu Feta (page 69)

1 cup (300 g) quartered artichoke hearts

1 cup (170 g) mixed whole olives

2 cups (100 g) pita chips (or gluten-free crackers, if necessary)

If you don't want to light the grill for the eggplant, you may carefully char the whole eggplant over a gas stove burner, holding it with tongs, for a similar smoky flavor.

"FISH" TACO BOWL

GLUTEN-FREE • SOY-FREE OPTION • NUT-FREE • SUGAR-FREE

Taco Tuesday is a weekly holiday that I celebrate regularly and for good reason—tacos are freakin' awesome! I will admit, however, that sometimes I'm not into getting my hands dirty from tortillas bursting at the seams with fillings, so this "Fish" Taco Bowl is a great alternative.

To make the cabbage slaw: Place all of the ingredients in a bowl, stir together until combined, and then refrigerate for 20 minutes.

To make the pico de gallo: Place all of the ingredients in a bowl, stir together until combined, and then refrigerate for 20 minutes.

To make the "fish": Preheat the oven to 350°F (176°C, or gas mark 4) and coat a baking sheet with a thin layer of oil or nonstick cooking spray.

In a mixing bowl, using two forks or your hands, pull apart the hearts of palm until they appear shredded. Stir in the lime juice, dulse flakes (see note on page 104), and salt until combined and then spread the mixture out on the baking sheet in a single layer. Bake for 12 to 15 minutes until the edges start to turn golden brown.

To assemble: While the "fish" is baking, place the tortilla strips on a baking sheet, brush with a thin layer of oil, and sprinkle with salt. Bake for 10 to 12 minutes until crispy.

Divide the slaw, pico de gallo, "fish," and tortillas among 4 shallow bowls, arranging the components in quadrants. Nestle the cilantro, jalapeño, and lime wedges in with the tortilla strips. Serve immediately.

YIELD: 4 servings

FOR THE CABBAGE SLAW:

1 cup (70 g) shredded red cabbage

1 cup (70 g) shredded green cabbage

1 cup (110 g) grated carrot

¼ cup (60 g) vegan mayonnaise (soy-free, if necessary)

1 teaspoon white vinegar

FOR THE PICO DE GALLO:

½ cup (90 g) diced tomato

⅓ cup (55 g) diced red onion

1 tablespoon (1 g) minced fresh cilantro

1 tablespoon (6 g) minced fresh jalapeño (optional)

½ teaspoon lime juice

Salt and freshly ground black pepper, to taste

FOR THE "FISH":

2 cans (14 ounces, or 400 g each) hearts of palm, drained

2 teaspoons lime juice

½ teaspoon dulse seaweed flakes

Pinch of salt

FOR THE ASSEMBLY:

4 small corn tortillas, cut into strips

¼ cup (4 g) loosely packed fresh cilantro leaves

2 tablespoons (11 g) sliced fresh jalapeño

8 lime wedges

MOLE BOWL-E

There are some recipes for which you use what seems like every pan in your kitchen, but the results make the cleanup so very much worth it. I warn you that this is one of those recipes: freekeh, sweet plantains, black beans, tempeh, and guacamole, topped off with a rich and flavorful mole sauce.

To make the mole sauce: Place the ancho chile in a small pot and cover with water, bring to a boil over medium heat, and cook for 10 minutes or until the pepper is very soft. Drain the chile, reserving ⅓ cup (80 ml) of the cooking water, and remove the stem from the chile.

Warm the coconut oil in a small pan over medium heat. Add the onion and garlic and sauté until translucent. In a blender, purée the onion, garlic, ancho chile, vegetable broth, chile cooking water, tomato sauce, dark chocolate, almond butter, cumin, chipotle chili powder, paprika, salt, and cinnamon until smooth.

Transfer the sauce to a large pan and simmer over medium-low heat for 15 minutes, whisking occasionally.

To make the freekeh: In a saucepan over medium heat, bring the freekeh and vegetable broth to a boil. Adjust the heat to medium-low and cook, covered, for 20 to 25 minutes.

When the freekeh is almost done cooking, melt the coconut oil in a large skillet over medium heat. Add the onion and bell pepper and sauté until the onions are translucent. Add the cooked freekeh to the skillet, along with the tomato sauce, Spanish olives, and capers. Adjust the heat to medium-low and cook for 5 minutes, stirring occasionally. Stir in the cilantro, salt, and pepper and reduce the heat to low to keep the freekeh warm.

(continued on next page)

FOR THE MOLE SAUCE:

1 dried ancho chile pepper

1 teaspoon coconut oil

½ cup (80 g) chopped white onion

1 clove of garlic, sliced

½ cup (120 ml) vegetable broth

2½ tablespoons (31 g) tomato sauce

2½ tablespoons (27 g) chopped dark chocolate (70 percent cacao)

1½ tablespoons (24 g) roasted almond butter

¾ teaspoon ground cumin

½ teaspoon ground chipotle chili powder

¼ teaspoon paprika

¼ teaspoon salt

⅛ teaspoon ground cinnamon

FOR THE FREEKEH:

⅔ cup (123 g) freekeh

1⅓ cups (315 ml) vegetable broth

1½ teaspoons coconut oil

½ cup (80 g) diced yellow onion

½ cup (75 g) diced green bell pepper

½ cup (123 g) tomato sauce

2 tablespoons (18 g) sliced Spanish olives

2 tablespoons (18 g) capers

1½ teaspoons minced fresh cilantro

½ teaspoon salt

Pinch of freshly ground black pepper

(continued from previous page)

To make the tempeh: Place the tempeh slab and vegetable broth in a small pan and bring to a boil over medium heat. Cover and cook for 10 minutes and then drain the tempeh. Cut the tempeh into cubes and then add them back into the pan along with the coconut oil. Brown each side over medium heat for 2 to 3 minutes. Season with salt and pepper.

To make the black beans: In a small pot over medium heat, melt the coconut oil and sauté the onion until translucent. Stir in the cumin and bay leaf and then empty the can of beans into the pot. Simmer over medium-low heat for 15 minutes or until the liquid reduces slightly. Season with the salt. Remove the bay leaf before serving.

To make the plantains: In a small skillet over medium heat, melt the coconut oil. Add the plantains to the skillet and caramelize the slices for 3 minutes on each side or until they are dark brown.

To assemble: Divide the freekeh, tempeh, black beans, plantains and Simple Guacamole among 4 bowls. Drizzle mole sauce over each bowl and serve hot.

YIELD: 4 servings

FOR THE TEMPEH:

8 ounces (225 g) tempeh

1 cup (235 ml) vegetable broth

1 teaspoon coconut oil

Salt and freshly ground black pepper, to taste

FOR THE BLACK BEANS:

1 teaspoon coconut oil

¼ cup (80 g) diced white onion

¾ teaspoon ground cumin

1 bay leaf

1 can (15 ounces, or 425 g) black beans, rinsed and drained

½ teaspoon salt

FOR THE PLANTAINS:

1 teaspoon coconut oil

1 large ripe plantain, sliced into ¼-inch-thick (6 mm) ovals

FOR THE ASSEMBLY:

1 batch of Simple Guacamole (page 198)

HOLIDAY HARVEST RISOTTO

GLUTEN-FREE • SOY-FREE • SUGAR-FREE

Risottos are creamy, rich, comforting, and make for a perfectly satiating winter meal. By adding puréed butternut squash to the mix, you can omit dairy and still get the same wonderful texture as a traditional risotto. This recipe is made even better by the addition of crispy sage leaves and toasted hazelnuts.

To make the squash: Preheat the oven to 375°F (190°C, or gas mark 5) and line a baking sheet with parchment paper.

Keeping the rind on, slice the squash into rounds, scooping the seeds out of each one.

Place the rounds onto the baking sheet and spray with a light coat of cooking oil. Sprinkle the salt and pepper over the slices and roast in the oven for 25 minutes, flipping the squash halfway through.

To make the risotto: While the squash is baking, heat the olive oil in a large saucepan over medium heat. Add the rice to the pan and toast the grains for 5 minutes or until they become translucent. Add the onion and sauté for 2 minutes and then add the garlic and cook for another 2 minutes. Reduce the heat to medium-low and add the vegetable broth to the rice, ½ cup (120 ml) at a time, each time waiting until the broth has been completely absorbed before adding more and stirring occasionally to prevent burning.

Once all of the broth has been used, which usually takes 15 to 20 minutes, add the nondairy milk, butternut squash purée, nutritional yeast, and dried sage to the rice and stir until combined. Simmer, covered, until the rice is fully cooked, just a few minutes longer, and then season with the salt, pepper, and nutmeg.

To make the garnish: In a small skillet over medium heat, heat the olive oil. Place the sage leaves in the skillet and fry for 3 to 4 minutes. Transfer to a paper towel to absorb excess oil.

(continued on next page)

FOR THE SQUASH:

1 pound (455 g) delicata squash

Cooking oil spray

¼ teaspoon salt

Pinch of freshly ground black pepper

FOR THE RISOTTO:

1 tablespoon (15 ml) olive oil

1 cup (192 g) Arborio rice

1 cup (160 g) diced yellow onion

2 cloves of garlic, minced

2½ cups (570 ml) gluten-free vegetable broth

1½ cups (355 ml) unsweetened soy-free nondairy milk

1½ cups (367 g) butternut squash purée

1 tablespoon (4 g) nutritional yeast

1 teaspoon ground sage

1 teaspoon salt, or to taste

¼ teaspoon freshly ground black pepper

⅛ teaspoon ground nutmeg

FOR THE GARNISH:

2 tablespoons (28 ml) olive oil

12 fresh sage leaves

½ cup (68 g) hazelnuts, toasted and chopped

(continued from previous page)

Divide the risotto among 4 bowls, along with the squash slices, and then top each one with fried sage leaves and toasted hazelnuts. Serve immediately.

YIELD: 4 servings

- You can either use canned butternut squash purée or make your own: Cut a butternut squash in half lengthwise, scoop out the seeds, place it cut side down in a baking dish, and bake at 350°F (180°C, or gas mark 4) for 40 minutes or until easily pierced with a fork. Let cool for 15 minutes and then scoop out the flesh.

- Toasting hazelnuts gives them a great texture and deeper flavor. Cook them in a small dry skillet over medium heat for 3 to 5 minutes until the skins darken.

ALOHA BOWL

NUT-FREE

Take an imaginary trip to the Hawaiian Islands with this bright bowl, inspired by popular, traditional Hawaiian dishes and ingredients such as poké, taro root, coleslaw, and teriyaki everything. Serve this meal with a refreshing mai tai, sit back, and relax.

To make the pineapple coleslaw: In a large bowl, toss all of the ingredients together. Refrigerate for at least 1 hour (this helps meld the flavors).

To make the tomato poké: Remove the seeds from the tomatoes and discard. Toss the tomatoes, scallions, liquid aminos, toasted sesame oil, dulse granules (see note on page 104), and red pepper flakes together in a bowl. Refrigerate for at least 1 hour (this helps meld the flavors).

To make the taro root fries: Preheat the oven to 400°F (200°C, or gas mark 6) and line a baking sheet with parchment paper or a silicone baking mat.

Toss the taro sticks with the melted coconut oil and salt and then place them on the baking sheet and bake for 30 minutes, flipping them halfway through. Once they have some golden edges, take them out and lightly sprinkle them with salt.

To make the rice: While the taro is roasting, place the rice and water in a small pot and bring to a boil over medium heat. Adjust the heat to medium-low, cover, and cook for 20 minutes or until soft.

(continued on next page)

If you are running short on time, you can use 8 ounces (227 g) of store-bought seitan, as well as premade teriyaki sauce, in place of the homemade versions.

FOR THE PINEAPPLE COLESLAW:

1 cup (155 g) diced fresh pineapple

1 cup (70 g) shredded red cabbage

1 cup (70 g) shredded white cabbage

½ cup (93 g) chopped orange

1 tablespoon (15 ml) white vinegar

1 teaspoon agave nectar

Salt and freshly ground black pepper, to taste

FOR THE TOMATO POKÉ:

1 pound (455 g) firm tomatoes, peeled and chopped

¼ cup (25 g) diced scallions

1 tablespoon (15 ml) liquid aminos or tamari

1 tablespoon (15 ml) toasted sesame oil

½ teaspoon dulse seaweed granules

½ teaspoon crushed red pepper flakes

FOR THE TARO ROOT FRIES:

1 pound (455 g) taro root, peeled and cut into matchsticks

1 tablespoon (14 g) coconut oil, melted

½ teaspoon salt

FOR THE RICE:

½ cup (98 g) white rice

1 cup (235 ml) water

(continued from previous page)

To make the teriyaki seitan: Place ¼ cup (60 ml) of the water, brown sugar, liquid aminos, agave nectar, ginger, and garlic in a large saucepan over medium heat. Bring to a boil and then adjust the heat to medium-low and simmer, uncovered, for 5 minutes.

While the sauce is simmering, heat a grill pan on the stovetop and grill the seitan for 2 minutes on each side or until there are visible char marks. Whisk the remaining ¼ cup (60 ml) of water with the cornstarch and add to the saucepan, whisking until combined. Keep cooking and whisking the sauce until it has thickened enough to coat the back of a spoon and then stir in the sesame seeds and toss the seitan into the pan, folding until coated evenly with the sauce.

Divide the coleslaw, poké, taro fries, rice, and teriyaki seitan among 4 bowls. Serve warm.

YIELD: 4 servings

FOR THE TERIYAKI SEITAN:

½ cup (120 ml) water, divided

2½ tablespoons (30 g) organic brown sugar

2 tablespoons (28 ml) liquid aminos or tamari

1 tablespoon (15 ml) agave nectar

½ teaspoon grated fresh ginger

½ teaspoon minced garlic

1 batch of Basic Seitan (page 196)

2 teaspoons cornstarch or arrowroot starch

1½ teaspoons sesame seeds

SUNNY GARDEN SAUTÉ WITH POLENTA

GLUTEN-FREE • SOY-FREE • NUT-FREE • SUGAR-FREE

Growing your own food has its own rewards, but when that is not a possibility, going to the farmers' market is the next best thing. Walking along the rows of tents, looking at the wide variety of colorful produce—especially during the summer—and having the aroma of fresh herbs, tomatoes, and more waft by you, is tantalizing. This bowl embodies all of that goodness.

To make the garden sauté: In a large skillet over medium heat, heat the olive oil. Sauté the shallots for 2 minutes and then add the green beans and cook for 5 minutes, stirring occasionally. (During this time, get started on the polenta.)

Add the radicchio, Swiss chard, tomatoes, white beans, and Italian seasoning to the skillet and sauté until the greens become wilted. Season with the salt and pepper.

To make the polenta: In a large pot over medium heat, bring the vegetable broth to a boil. Stir the polenta into the broth, adjust the heat to medium-low, and cook until the polenta is soft and creamy, about 15 to 20 minutes. Season with salt.

Divide the polenta among 4 bowls, top with the garden sauté, and serve.

YIELD: 4 servings

FOR THE GARDEN SAUTÉ:

1 teaspoon olive oil

3 shallots, sliced

6 ounces (170 g) green beans, ends trimmed and chopped

1 small head of radicchio, chopped

¼ pound (115 g) Swiss chard, chopped

1 pound (455 g) tomatoes, chopped

1 can (15 ounces, or 425 g) white beans, rinsed and drained

½ teaspoon dried Italian seasoning

1 teaspoon salt, or to taste

¼ teaspoon freshly ground black pepper, or to taste

FOR THE POLENTA:

3 cups (700 ml) gluten-free vegetable broth

1 cup (140 g) polenta grits (I use Bob's Red Mill.)

Salt, to taste

GLAZED PORTOBELLO PESTO PASTA BOWL

GLUTEN-FREE OPTION • SOY-FREE • SUGAR-FREE

In this recipe, fresh basil pesto coats comforting pasta, which contrasts in flavor to the meaty sweetness of balsamic-glazed portobello mushrooms. It's all topped by crunchy pine nuts, beautiful cherry tomatoes, and a pinch of truffle salt.

To make the balsamic-glazed portobellos: Place the mushroom slices in a shallow container with an airtight lid. Pour the water, balsamic vinegar, salt, and pepper into the container, swish it around, and marinate in the refrigerator for 2 hours.

Heat a large pan over medium heat and add ¼ cup (60 ml) of the marinade. Bring to a simmer and then add the mushroom slices to the pan, cooking for 5 minutes on each side or until all the marinade has reduced and the mushrooms have browned.

To make the pasta: Cook the pasta according to the package instructions, leaving it just a little firmer than you normally would. Drain the noodles, return them to the pot, and set over medium-low heat. Stir the Pesto into the pasta until coated evenly, cook for 2 minutes, and season with the salt.

To assemble: Divide the pasta among 4 bowls, along with the portobello slices. Top each bowl with cherry tomatoes, pine nuts, and a small pinch of truffle salt, if using. Serve immediately.

YIELD: 4 servings

FOR THE BALSAMIC-GLAZED PORTOBELLOS:

4 large portobello mushroom caps, thickly sliced

1 cup (235 ml) water

½ cup (120 ml) balsamic vinegar

1 teaspoon salt

½ teaspoon freshly ground black pepper

FOR THE PASTA:

3 cups (315 g) whole wheat pasta (or brown rice pasta, if gluten-free)

1 batch of Pesto (page 51)

½ teaspoon salt, or to taste

FOR THE ASSEMBLY:

1 cup (150 g) halved cherry tomatoes

¼ cup (35 g) pine nuts

Truffle salt, for sprinkling (optional)

SEITAN SATAY BOWL WITH PEANUT SAUCE

Food on sticks makes for the best eats, especially when those sticks are lemongrass skewers and the food is seitan satay covered in a creamy peanut sauce and served with citrusy jasmine rice, cucumber salad, and sautéed kale.

To make the satay marinade: Place the seitan strips in a shallow container with a lid. In a saucepan over medium heat, whisk the coconut milk, peanut butter, soy sauce, brown sugar, chili paste, garlic, ginger, and curry powder and cook for 3 minutes.

Pour the satay sauce over the seitan strips and place the container in the refrigerator to marinate for 2 hours.

To make the cucumber salad: Toss all of the ingredients together in a small bowl and refrigerate for 30 minutes before serving.

To make the lemongrass lime rice: In a large pot over medium heat, bring the rice, coconut milk, water, lemongrass, lime zest, and salt to a boil. Adjust the heat to medium-low, cover, and cook for 25 to 30 minutes until all of the liquid has been absorbed and the rice is fully cooked. Fluff with a wooden spoon and keep covered. Remove the lemongrass stalks when ready to serve.

(continued on next page)

FOR THE SATAY MARINADE:

1 batch of Basic Seitan (page 196); formed into 8 thin strips for skewering

⅓ cup (80 ml) full-fat coconut milk

1 tablespoon (16 g) creamy peanut butter

1 tablespoon (15 ml) soy sauce

2 teaspoons organic brown sugar

1 teaspoon sambal chili paste

1 clove of garlic, minced

1 teaspoon grated fresh ginger

½ teaspoon yellow curry powder

FOR THE CUCUMBER SALAD:

½ pound (225 g) cucumbers, sliced into ¼-inch (6 mm) -thick rounds

½ cup (80 g) slivered red onion

1 tablespoon (15 ml) rice vinegar

FOR THE LEMONGRASS LIME RICE:

1 cup (184 g) jasmine rice

1 can (13.6 ounces, or 380 ml) lite coconut milk

½ cup (120 ml) water

4 pieces (3 inches, or 7.5 cm) lemongrass, scored

1 teaspoon grated lime zest

Pinch of salt

(continued from previous page)

To make the sautéed kale: Heat the coconut oil in a large skillet over medium heat. Sauté the ginger and garlic for 1 minute and then add the kale to the skillet and sauté for 3 to 5 minutes, until the kale has wilted but is still bright green. Season with salt and pepper.

To make the peanut sauce: Whisk all of the ingredients together until smooth.

To make the seitan satay: Prepare a hot fire in a grill (375°F, or 190°C) and oil the grill grates. Peel layers off the lemongrass pieces until they are about ¼ inch (6 mm) in diameter. Skewer the seitan with the lemongrass and grill for 3 to 5 minutes on each side, basting with satay marinade while grilling.

To assemble: Divide the lemongrass lime rice, cucumber salad, and sautéed kale among 4 bowls. Place 2 seitan skewers in each bowl, drizzle with peanut sauce, and top with crushed peanuts. Serve immediately.

YIELD: 4 servings

FOR THE SAUTÉED KALE:

1½ teaspoons coconut oil

2 teaspoons grated fresh ginger

1 clove of garlic, minced

1 bunch (6 ounces, or 170 g) of lacinato kale, stems removed and chopped

Salt and freshly ground black pepper, to taste

FOR THE PEANUT SAUCE:

3 tablespoons (48 g) creamy peanut butter, heated

3 tablespoons (45 ml) full-fat coconut milk

1½ tablespoons (23 ml) rice vinegar

1 tablespoon (15 ml) soy sauce

1½ teaspoons sambal chili paste

FOR THE ASSEMBLY:

8 pieces (7 inches, or 17.5 cm) lemongrass

¼ cup (36 g) crushed roasted peanuts

SUMMER PICNIC BOWL

GLUTEN-FREE • NUT-FREE

This bowl right here reminds me of so many summer barbecues and parties that I have been to over the years. My mom always made the best baked beans, while my dad was all over the potato salad—even though it was store bought—and how can you go wrong with slices of juicy watermelon?

To make the baked beans: Preheat the oven to 350°F (180°C, or gas mark 4).

In an 8-inch (20 cm) square baking dish, or a bean pot if you have one, stir all of the ingredients together. Bake, uncovered, for 30 minutes. Remove from the oven and cover to keep warm.

To make the Cajun tofu: Turn the oven temperature to 400°F (200°C, or gas mark 6) and line a baking sheet with parchment paper.

Wrap each block of tofu in a clean kitchen towel. Set them on a plate and stack some heavy objects on them (in a stable manner). Wait 15 minutes for the moisture to be pressed out.

Place the salt, paprika, garlic powder, celery seed, black pepper, cumin, coriander, onion powder, red pepper flakes, oregano, cinnamon, and dill in a spice or coffee grinder and pulse until combined.

(continued on next page)

FOR THE BAKED BEANS:

2 cans (15 ounces, or 425 g, each) white beans, rinsed and drained

¾ cup (188 g) Strawberry Barbecue Sauce (page 193) or your favorite vegan barbecue sauce

¼ cup (40 g) diced white onion

¼ cup (115 g) chopped Tempting Tempeh Bacon (page 198)

2 tablespoons (24 g) organic brown sugar

2 tablespoons (28 ml) maple syrup

⅛ teaspoon salt

FOR THE CAJUN TOFU:

2 packages (12 ounces, or 340 g each) extra-firm tofu, rinsed and drained

2 teaspoons salt

1 teaspoon paprika

½ teaspoon garlic powder

¼ teaspoon celery seed

¼ teaspoon freshly ground black pepper

¼ teaspoon ground cumin

¼ teaspoon ground coriander

¼ teaspoon onion powder

¼ teaspoon crushed red pepper flakes

¼ teaspoon dried oregano

Pinch of ground cinnamon

Pinch of dried dill

(continued from previous page)

Slice each block of tofu into 6 rectangles, place them on the lined baking sheet, and rub the spice mixture on each side of each piece of tofu. Bake for 10 minutes and then flip the pieces and bake for another 10 minutes. Turn the broiler on and broil both sides for 5 minutes each.

To assemble: Divide the baked beans and Tex-Mex Potato Salad among 4 bowls and then place 2 slices of watermelon and 3 slices of tofu in each bowl. Serve immediately.

YIELD: 4 serving

FOR THE ASSEMBLY:

½ of a batch of Tex-Mex Potato Salad (page 88)

8 slices of watermelon

RAW CRUNCH BOWL

GLUTEN-FREE • SOY-FREE • SUGAR-FREE

Spiralizing vegetables into noodles is something I love to do when I am looking to have a healthy, easy meal with tons of crunch to it. These mixed veggie noodles are slathered in a creamy almond and red pepper sauce and topped with raw salted almonds.

To make the creamy pepper sauce: In a blender, place all of the ingredients and purée until very smooth. Set aside.

To make the almond topping: Chop the almonds, place them in a small bowl, and toss with the salt and pepper.

For the veggie noodles: In a large bowl, toss the different vegetable noodles together and then divide them among 4 large bowls. Drizzle the creamy pepper sauce over each bowl, finish with the almond topping and a couple of basil leaves, and serve.

YIELD: 4 servings

> Here's a fun way to peel almonds: Once they are soaked and drained, squeeze them between your thumb and index finger at the round end of the nut. The almond will quite easily shoot out of the skin through the pointy end.

FOR THE CREAMY PEPPER SAUCE:

½ cup (73 g) raw almonds, soaked in warm water for 2 hours, drained, and peeled

2 cups (300 g) chopped red bell pepper

¼ cup (60 ml) water

1 tablespoon (15 ml) apple cider vinegar

1 clove of garlic, peeled

½ teaspoon salt

¼ teaspoon freshly ground black pepper

FOR THE ALMOND TOPPING:

½ cup (73 g) raw almonds, soaked in warm water for 2 hours and peeled

¼ teaspoon salt

Pinch of freshly ground black pepper

FOR THE VEGGIE NOODLES:

½ pound (225 g) zucchini, sliced on a spiralizer

½ pound (225 g) yellow squash, sliced on a spiralizer

¼ pound (115 g) rainbow carrots, sliced on a spiralizer

Fresh basil leaves, for garnish

KIMCHI BOWL WITH RED CURRY ALMOND SAUCE

GLUTEN-FREE • SOY-FREE OPTION

Kimchi is not only extremely tasty, but its probiotic qualities also help your gut health. In this bowl, the kimchi is nestled among brown rice, broccoli, adzuki beans, and a spicy red curry almond sauce; it's a flavor explosion!

To make the bowl: Place the rice and water in a rice cooker (that has a steamer basket) and cook for 20 minutes or until the rice is soft. For the last 5 minutes of the rice cooking, place the broccoli florets in the steamer basket and cook until bright green and slightly crunchy.

In a small pot over medium heat, mix the adzuki beans with the liquid aminos and cook for 2 to 3 minutes.

To make the red curry almond sauce: Whisk all of the ingredients together until smooth.

To assemble: Divide the rice and broccoli among 4 bowls. Divide the adzuki beans among the bowls. Place one-quarter of the kimchi in each bowl and drizzle the red curry almond sauce over the top. Garnish with the black sesame seeds and serve.

YIELD: 4 servings

FOR THE BOWL:

1 cup (184 g) long-grain brown rice

2 cups (245 ml) water

½ pound (225 g) broccoli florets

1 can (15 ounces, or 425 g) adzuki beans, rinsed and drained

1 tablespoon (15 ml) liquid aminos

FOR THE RED CURRY ALMOND SAUCE:

2½ tablespoons (38 ml) water

2 tablespoons (32 g) almond butter

2 teaspoons red curry paste

1 to 2 tablespoons (15 to 20 ml) lime juice

FOR THE ASSEMBLY:

1 cup (170 g) store-bought vegan kimchi

2 tablespoons (16 g) black sesame seeds

Chapter 6

DAMN GOOD DESSERT BOWLS

BECAUSE AWESOME TREATS ARE NOT JUST FOR HOLIDAYS

If I had to choose between brunch and dessert dishes for my favorite food category, desserts would win by just a hair. Though there are many delicious desserts that do not come in bowl form, these ambrosial recipes will convert you into a sweet-treat bowl lover!

AMARETTO CHERRY ICE CREAM

GLUTEN-FREE

Booze plus dessert is one heavenly combination that is hard to mess up. But it is even easier to make right when the recipe includes beautiful dark, sweet cherries and an ultra-creamy ice cream.

To make the boozy cherry sauce: Place all of the ingredients in a small pan over medium heat and bring to a simmer, uncovered. Adjust the heat to medium-low and simmer for 15 to 20 minutes, stirring occasionally. You want the cherries to be soft and breaking apart a bit. The sauce should coat a spoon once it has cooled slightly. Transfer the sauce to a small bowl and refrigerate.

To make the ice cream base: Drain and rinse the cashews. Place the soy milk and cashews in a high-speed blender and purée until completely smooth. Add the rest of the ice cream ingredients to the mixture and purée until smooth; you will see specks of cherry skins, which is fine.

To assemble: Pour the base into an ice cream maker and churn for 25 minutes or until thick but not frozen solid. In the meantime, prepare a 9 x 5 x 3-inch (23 x 13 x 7.5 cm) loaf pan by lining it with parchment paper.

When the ice cream base is ready, take the cherry sauce out of the refrigerator. Begin filling the loaf pan, alternating layers of the base and the cherry sauce and making 4 layers of the base and 3 thinner layers of sauce. Drag a butter knife through the mixtures to create swirls.

Place the ice cream in the freezer for 1 to 2 hours. When you are ready to serve, take the ice cream out and let soften for 5 to 10 minutes before scooping, if necessary. Garnish with fresh cherry pieces, if using, and serve in small bowls.

YIELD: 6 servings

FOR THE BOOZY CHERRY SAUCE:

1 pound (455 g) dark sweet cherries, pitted

½ cup (115 ml) amaretto

2 tablespoons (24 g) organic brown sugar

FOR THE ICE CREAM BASE:

1½ cups (210 g) raw cashews, soaked in warm water for 1 hour

1½ cups (355 ml) unsweetened plain soy milk

⅔ cup (103 g) dark sweet cherries, pitted

5 to 6 tablespoons (75 to 90 ml) maple syrup

2 to 3 teaspoons (10 to 15 ml) amaretto

⅛ teaspoon salt

Dark sweet cherries, pitted and chopped (optional)

> If you do not have an ice cream maker, pour the base into a gallon (3.7 L)-size zip-top plastic bag, lay it flat, and freeze it until hard (about 1 hour). Then break it into smaller pieces and place the pieces into a food processor; process with an s-blade until smooth.

PLUOT BALSAMIC SORBET

GLUTEN-FREE • SOY-FREE • NUT-FREE

This slightly tart, summery sorbet is as refreshing as it is easy to make. There's no ice cream maker needed for this recipe!

To make the pluot sorbet: Place the frozen pluot slices, sugar, and balsamic vinegar in a food processor and pulse until they are combined and smooth. Transfer the mixture to a freezer-safe container and freeze for 45 to 60 minutes.

To make the balsamic reduction: Heat the balsamic vinegar in a small sauté pan over medium heat. Simmer for 7 to 10 minutes, until the vinegar has reduced enough to coat the back of a spoon (it will thicken slightly as it cools).

When the sorbet is hard enough to scoop, divide it among 4 bowls and drizzle with the balsamic reduction.

YIELD: 4 servings

FOR THE PLUOT SORBET:

2 pounds (910 g) pluots, sliced and frozen on a baking sheet

¼ cup (48 g) organic cane sugar

2 tablespoons (28 ml) balsamic vinegar

FOR THE BALSAMIC REDUCTION:

¼ cup (60 ml) balsamic vinegar

ROASTED PEACH PARFAIT WITH CRUMBLE AND WHISKEY BUTTERCREAM

SOY-FREE • NUT-FREE

There is no way around it: This dessert is rich, decadent, and something I imagine eating whilst sitting on a porch in the South during the months of summer. Maybe it is the roasted peaches or maybe it is the splash of sweet whiskey in the buttercream; either way, this parfait is quite the treat.

To make the shortbread crumble: In a small bowl, stir together the flaxseed and hot water and let sit for 5 minutes. Using a stand or handheld electric mixer, whip the sugar and coconut oil on high speed until combined. With the mixer on, add the flaxseed mixture, nondairy milk, and vanilla and beat until fluffy.

Sift together the flour, baking powder, and salt. Add the dry mixture to the wet mixture and mix on medium speed until the cookie dough is crumbly but sticks together when pressed or squeezed. Form into a dough ball and refrigerate for 10 minutes.

Preheat the oven to 350°F (180°C, or gas mark 4) and line a large baking sheet with a silicone baking mat or parchment paper. Lightly flour your workspace and rolling pin and roll out the cookie dough to ¼ inch (6 mm) thick.

Using a 2½ inch (6.5 cm)-round cookie cutter, cut out cookies and place them on the baking sheet, kneading leftover scraps and repeating the cutting process. Bake the cookies for 10 to 12 minutes until they are lightly golden. Place the cookies on a cooling rack. They will further harden as they cool. Leave the oven on.

(continued on next page)

FOR THE SHORTBREAD CRUMBLE:

1½ teaspoons ground flaxseed

1 tablespoon (15 ml) hot water

¼ cup (48 g) organic cane sugar

¼ cup (56 g) coconut oil

1½ teaspoons unsweetened soy-free, nut-free nondairy milk

½ teaspoon vanilla extract

¾ cup (94 g) unbleached all-purpose flour

¼ teaspoon baking powder

Pinch of salt

FOR THE WHISKEY BUTTERCREAM:

½ cup (112 g) soy-free vegan butter, near room temperature

1 tablespoon (20 g) vegan honey (such as Bee Free Honee) or (15 ml) agave nectar

1½ cups (180 g) organic powdered sugar

1 tablespoon (15 ml) fruit-flavored whiskey (I use cherry whiskey.)

(continued from previous page)

To make the whiskey buttercream: Whip the vegan butter in a bowl with a handheld electric mixer; add the vegan honey and whip until combined. Slowly, add ½ cup (60 g) powdered sugar at a time to the whipped butter while mixing on medium-high speed until all the sugar is incorporated and the buttercream is smooth.

Add the whiskey and whip until combined. Place the bowl in the refrigerator to chill for 15 to 20 minutes.

To assemble: Line a baking sheet with parchment paper. Place the peach slices on the baking sheet and roast for 25 minutes. Let cool slightly on a cooling rack.

Divide half of the peaches among 4 small glass bowls and then crumble 1 shortbread cookie into each bowl. Top the crumbles with the whiskey buttercream. Layer the remaining peaches in each bowl, top with 1 short-bread cookie, whiskey buttercream, and a drizzle of vegan honey to top it off. Serve immediately.

YIELD: **4 servings**

FOR THE ASSEMBLY:

1 pound (455 g) peaches, pitted and sliced

Vegan honey, for drizzling

> This dessert would also be great with roasted blackberries during the spring, especially with a little fresh mint added for garnish.

MEXICAN CHOCOLATE CRÈME BRÛLÉE WITH CANDIED MANGO

GLUTEN-FREE • SOY-FREE • NUT-FREE

I was given the challenge of creating an incredible vegan crème brûlée recipe for a restaurant a couple of years ago. Ever since then, I cannot help trying out all kinds of flavor combinations and enjoying each immensely. This time, it's a spicy chocolate crème with sweet candied mango on top.

(continued on next page)

(continued from previous page)

To make the crème brûlée: Preheat the oven to 325°F (170°C, or gas mark 3). Place all of the ingredients in a blender and purée for at least 30 seconds, making sure there are no powdery chunks in the liquid. Pour the mixture into a small saucepan, set over medium-low heat, and bring to a simmer.

Whisk the mixture continuously until it thickens, without becoming chunky, about 2 minutes. It should be thick enough to stick to a spoon and look like a smooth gravy. It is crucial that the cornstarch breaks down and thickens, but be careful not to let it overcook in the saucepan.

Place four 2 ounce (60 ml) ramekins inside a casserole dish. Fill the casserole dish with water until it is halfway up the outside of the ramekins. Carefully pour the crème mixture into each ramekin and transfer the dish to the oven, making sure not to splash the water.

Bake for 25 minutes until there is just a tiny jiggle when you lightly bump the casserole dish. Transfer the casserole dish to a cooling rack.

Once the ramekins are cool enough to touch, remove them from the dish, place them on a cooling rack, and refrigerate for 1 to 2 hours. When you want to serve them, sprinkle 1 to 2 teaspoons sugar on top of the crème. Using a kitchen torch or the broiler, melt the sugar until it reaches a light brown/orange color, or darker if you prefer.

To make the candied mango: Place the strips of mango in the bottom of a skillet, sprinkle them with the sugar, and pour the water over them. Bring the mixture to a boil and then adjust heat to medium-low for and cook for 10 to 15 minutes, stirring occasionally, until the mixture is syrupy and bubbling, without much liquid left. Carefully take the mango strips out of the skillet and place them on wax paper on a cooling rack. You can refrigerate them until you are ready to serve the crème brûlée.

When ready to serve, shake a light dusting of cayenne pepper over the caramelized sugar crust and top with a few pieces of candied mango.

YIELD: 4 servings

FOR THE CRÈME BRÛLÉE:

⅔ cup (160 ml) full-fat coconut milk

⅓ cup (80 ml) water

5 tablespoons (60 g) organic cane sugar, plus more for sprinkling

¼ cup (22 g) unsweetened cocoa powder

1½ tablespoons (12 g) tapioca starch

1 tablespoon (8 g) cornstarch

¼ teaspoon cayenne pepper

⅛ teaspoon ground chipotle chili powder

Pinch of Indian black salt (kala namak)

FOR THE CANDIED MANGO:

¼ cup (30 g) dried unsweetened mango, cut into 1-inch (2.5 cm) strips

2 tablespoons (24 g) organic cane sugar

¼ cup (60 ml) water

Cayenne pepper, for dusting

> To make it easier to torch or broil the sugar crust, I suggest putting the sugar into a food processor and grinding it finer, so that it melts more easily.

RAW APPLE CRISP

GLUTEN-FREE • SOY-FREE

Apples and cinnamon are a food combination that is popular and undeniably delectable. With this raw apple crisp, we take what is often a heavy dessert and make it light, with more nutrients, while keeping the flavors intact.

To make the apple filling: In a large bowl, toss all of the ingredients together until evenly coated. Divide the apple mixture among 4 small bowls.

To make the crisp topping: Place the buckwheat groats, almonds, and dates in a food processor and pulse until the mixture resembles coarse sand. Add the coconut oil and salt to the mixture and pulse until incorporated. Sprinkle over the apple filling in each bowl.

Add another delicious layer to this raw dessert by drizzling Date Caramel on top.

YIELD: 4 servings

FOR THE APPLE FILLING:

1 pound (455 g) green or pink apples, cored and thinly sliced

1 tablespoon (9 g) coconut sugar

1 teaspoon agave nectar

1 teaspoon ground cinnamon

Pinch of salt

FOR THE CRISP TOPPING:

½ cup (92 g) raw buckwheat groats

¼ cup (36 g) raw almonds (optional to soak in warm water for 2 hours)

⅓ cup (59 g) Medjool dates, pitted

1 tablespoon (14 g) coconut oil, melted

¼ teaspoon salt

Date Caramel (page 200), for topping (optional)

NO-BAKE BERRY CHEESECAKE

GLUTEN-FREE • SOY-FREE

Here is a cute dessert that has all of the creaminess and tang of cheesecake, along with a juicy berry topping and a crunchy raw crust, without all of the baking and waiting. These small, sweet bowls are definitely crowd-pleasers!

To make the crust: Place all of the ingredients in a food processor and pulse until the mixture resembles coarse sand. Pour into a bowl and set aside.

To make the cheesecake filling: Drain and rinse the cashews. Place all of the ingredients in a high-speed blender and purée until completely smooth. Chill in the refrigerator until ready to assemble.

To make the berry topping: In a small pan over medium heat, bring all of the ingredients to a boil. Adjust the heat to medium-low and simmer for 7 to 10 minutes, stirring occasionally, until the berries have broken down and the mixture thickens.

Place 2 tablespoons (16 g) of the crust into the bottom of each small glass serving bowl. Push down gently on the crust to compact it. Next, carefully spoon 5 to 6 tablespoons (75 to 90 g) of the cheesecake filling into each bowl; tap down lightly to settle the filling.

You can chill the glasses for 10 minutes before completing the last step, but it's not necessary; it will just make the filling firmer for the topping to sit upon. Last, spoon 2 to 3 tablespoons (28 to 45 g) of berry topping into each glass. Chill for 30 minutes before serving.

YIELD: 4 servings

FOR THE CRUST MIX:

¼ cup (36 g) raw almonds

¼ cup (45 g) Medjool dates, pitted

Pinch of salt

FOR THE CHEESECAKE FILLING:

1½ cups (210 g) raw cashews, soaked in warm water for 30 minutes

½ cup (120 ml) water

¼ cup (60 g) plain coconut milk yogurt

3 tablespoons (45 ml) maple syrup

1 tablespoon (15 ml) lemon juice

Pinch of salt

FOR THE BERRY TOPPING:

¾ cup (109 g) fresh blackberries

¾ cup (109 g) fresh blueberries

3 tablespoons (27 g) coconut sugar

2 tablespoons (28 ml) water

MINT CHOCOLATE CHIP DOUGHNUT SUNDAE

SOY-FREE • NUT-FREE

Why eat a brownie sundae when you can have a doughnut sundae? A warm, pillowy doughnut, coated with mint glaze, chocolate sauce, and a heaping scoop of vegan mint chip ice cream. You are going to need a post-dessert pillow for all of the sweet dreams that you'll be having.

To make the doughnuts: In a glass cup or bowl, stir together the yeast, warm nondairy milk, water, and sugar with a plastic or wooden spoon. Let the yeast proof for 10 minutes and then stir in the melted coconut oil and aquafaba.

Sift the flour into a large bowl and fold in the yeast mixture. Knead until fully combined and then cover the bowl with a kitchen towel and let the dough rise for 60 minutes in a warm area.

Preheat a deep fryer or deep cast-iron skillet filled with 1 inch (2.5 cm) of oil to 375°F (190°C). Once the dough has risen, dust your work surface with flour and roll the dough out about 1 inch (2.5 cm) thick. Use a doughnut cutter, or a 3-inch (7.5 mm) and a 1-inch (2.5 cm) cutter, to cut 4 doughnut shapes from the dough. Separate the doughnut holes, a.k.a. pre-sundae snacks, for frying later.

Carefully, place 1 doughnut into the fryer at a time, frying for 1 minute on each side. Scoop the doughnut out of the fryer, letting the oil drip off, and place it on a plate lined with paper towels. Repeat until all the doughnuts (and doughnut holes) are fried.

(continued on next page)

FOR THE DOUGHNUTS:

½ teaspoon active dry yeast

6 tablespoons (90 ml) unsweetened soy-free, nut-free nondairy milk, warmed

1 tablespoon (15 ml) water

2 tablespoons (24 g) organic cane sugar

2 tablespoons (28 g) coconut oil, melted

1 tablespoon (15 ml) aquafaba (the liquid drained from a can of chickpeas—see note on page 114)

1¼ cups (156 g) unbleached all-purpose flour

Mild-flavored oil, for frying

FOR THE MINT GLAZE:

½ cup (60 g) sifted organic powdered sugar

1 tablespoon (14 g) coconut oil, melted

1 tablespoon (15 ml) unsweetened soy-free, nut-free nondairy milk

½ teaspoon mint extract

FOR THE ASSEMBLY:

4 scoops soy-free, nut-free vegan mint chocolate chip ice cream

Chocolate Sauce (page 199)

2 tablespoons (12 g) minced fresh mint

(continued from previous page)

To make the glaze: In a small bowl, vigorously whisk the powdered sugar, melted coconut oil, nondairy milk, and mint extract until smooth. Drizzle it over the tops of the warm doughnuts.

To assemble: Place a doughnut in each of the four bowls and then place a scoop of ice cream onto each one. Drizzle with Chocolate Sauce and top with minced mint leaves. Serve immediately.

YIELD: 4 servings

Halve the size of the doughnuts, when cutting them out, as well as the scoops of ice cream when plating, and you can make this into the perfect party dessert bowl!

STRAWBERRIES AND CREAM HUSH PUPPIES

GLUTEN-FREE • SOY-FREE

If you aren't familiar with hush puppies, they are basically little balls of fried cornbread, and they are amazing in both savory and sweet versions. In this particular recipe, the hush puppies are gluten-free, dotted with fresh strawberries, and drizzled with a sweet vanilla cream.

Preheat a deep fryer, or a deep cast-iron skillet filled with 1½ inches (3.8 cm) of oil to 375°F (190°C).

In a large bowl, sift together the cornmeal, gluten-free flour, sugar, baking powder, and salt.

In a smaller bowl, combine the nondairy milk, aquafaba, and vanilla. Add the wet mixture to the dry mixture and stir until there are no dry pockets; fold in the strawberries and let the batter sit for 10 minutes to thicken.

Using a 1-ounce (28 ml) scoop, scoop 4 to 6 hush puppies into the oil and fry for 5 minutes, flipping over halfway through, or until they are golden brown. Remove the cooked hush puppies from the oil with a slotted spoon and place them on a plate lined with paper towels to soak up the excess oil. Repeat the process until all of the batter is used up.

Divide the hush puppies among 6 small bowls, drizzle each one with Sweet Cashew Cream, and sprinkle with vanilla powder. Serve immediately.

YIELD: 6 servings

Mild-flavored cooking oil, for frying

2 cups (275 g) cornmeal

¼ cup (34 g) gluten-free all-purpose flour

6 tablespoons (72 g) organic cane sugar

1 tablespoon (14 g) baking powder

½ teaspoon salt

¾ cup (180 ml) unsweetened soy-free nondairy milk

¼ cup (60 ml) aquafaba (the liquid drained from a can of chickpeas—see note on page 114)

1 teaspoon vanilla extract

1 cup (170 g) diced fresh strawberries

1 cup (235 ml) Sweet Cashew Cream (page 200)

1 teaspoon vanilla powder

BRITTLE DRIZZLE AND BANANAS WITH COCONUT ICE CREAM

GLUTEN-FREE • SOY-FREE

Ultra-luscious coconut ice cream covered in a sweet drizzle that turns crunchy and topped with caramelized bananas—is your mouth watering yet?

To make the ice cream: Place the coconut milk, coconut flakes, coconut sugar, vanilla, and salt in a blender and purée until completely smooth. Pour the mixture into an ice cream maker and churn for 25 minutes. Transfer the ice cream to the freezer.

To make the caramelized bananas: Heat the oil in a large skillet over medium heat. Add the bananas to the skillet and sprinkle the brown sugar and allspice over them. Cook for 3 to 4 minutes on each side until caramelized; adjust the heat to low to keep warm until ready to serve.

To make the brittle drizzle: In a large pan, stir the coconut milk, sugar, vanilla, and salt together over medium heat. Bring to a simmer, whisking occasionally, and cook until the mixture becomes smooth and tan in color and is pulling away from the edges of the pan to become a singular blob.

Divide the ice cream among 4 bowls, topping each one with caramelized bananas and the brittle drizzle. Add an extra shake of allspice and serve immediately.

YIELD: 4 servings

FOR THE COCONUT ICE CREAM:

1 can (13.5 ounces, or 380 ml) full-fat coconut milk

1 cup (60 g) unsweetened large coconut flakes

¼ cup (36 g) coconut sugar

1 teaspoon vanilla extract

¼ teaspoon salt

FOR THE CARAMELIZED BANANAS:

2 teaspoons coconut oil

2 medium bananas, peeled and cut into ½-inch (6 mm) -thick oval slices

2 tablespoons (24 g) organic brown sugar

⅛ teaspoon ground allspice, plus more for garnish

FOR THE BRITTLE DRIZZLE:

6 tablespoons (90 ml) full-fat coconut milk

½ cup (96 g) organic sugar

1 teaspoon vanilla extract

⅛ teaspoon salt

PUMPKIN SPICE AFFOGATO

GLUTEN-FREE • SOY-FREE • NUT-FREE

When leaves start falling, pumpkin becomes all the rage, along with pumpkin-spiced everything, the most notorious example being the pumpkin spice latte. But why have a latte when you can combine your caffeine intake with a spiced ice cream that actually has pumpkin in it?

Place the coconut milk, pumpkin purée, brown sugar, vanilla, cinnamon, salt, cloves, ginger, and nutmeg into a blender and purée until completely smooth. Pour the mixture into an ice cream maker and churn for 25 minutes. Transfer the ice cream to the freezer.

Once firm enough to scoop, divide the ice cream among 4 bowls. Serve a shot of espresso with each one so that each person can pour the hot espresso over the ice cream and enjoy immediately.

YIELD: 4 servings

1 can (13.5 ounces, or 380 ml) full-fat coconut milk

1 cup (245 g) canned plain puréed pumpkin

½ cup (96 g) organic brown sugar

1 teaspoon vanilla extract

1 teaspoon ground cinnamon

½ teaspoon salt

¼ teaspoon ground cloves

¼ teaspoon ground ginger

⅛ teaspoon ground nutmeg

4 shots of brewed espresso

FANCY FRUIT BOWL

GLUTEN-FREE • SOY-FREE • NUT-FREE

Do not be intimidated by the recipe title: This fruit bowl is fancy in its elements alone but is quite fun and easy to put together. Chocolate-dipped figs, fancy golden raisins, and grilled oranges make for a luxurious dessert.

Line a baking sheet or plate with wax paper. Pat the outside of the figs dry (so the coating sticks) and dip them into the Chocolate Sauce, using a spoon for fuller coverage if needed. Let the excess sauce drip off and set the figs on the wax paper; immediately sprinkle each one with a few grains of coarse salt, and place the plate in the freezer to set the chocolate.

In a blender, purée the rolled oats, water, maple syrup, vanilla, cardamom, and salt until completely smooth. Keep the mixture in blender while grilling the oranges.

Heat a grill pan over medium heat and coat it with coconut oil. Peel the oranges, slice each into 4 rounds, and grill the slices for 4 to 5 minutes on each side until there are visibly dark grill marks.

Place 2 grilled orange slices in each of the 4 bowls and then divide the chocolate-covered figs and golden raisins among the bowls. Run the blender for 30 seconds and then drizzle the creamy oat sauce over each dessert. Serve immediately.

YIELD: 4 servings

½ pound (225 g) Mission figs

Chocolate Sauce (page 199)

Coarse salt, for sprinkling

½ cup (48 g) gluten-free rolled oats

½ cup (120 ml) water

5 tablespoons (75 ml) maple syrup

1 teaspoon vanilla extract

¼ teaspoon ground cardamom

Pinch of salt

2 large oranges

Coconut oil, for the grill pan

½ cup (75 g) golden raisins

S'MORES PUDDING BOWL

SOY-FREE • NUT-FREE

Want to capture the essence of the summer season and put it in a bowl? I have the solution! This s'mores pudding bowl utilizes the ever-fascinating aquafaba (the brine drained from a can of chickpeas), crushed grahams, and a rich avocado-based chocolate pudding.

To make the chocolate pudding: Place all of the ingredients in a food processor and process with an s-blade until smooth. It may take a couple of minutes for the dates to break down. Add more date soaking water to the pudding if you think it is too thick. Refrigerate the pudding for 1 to 2 hours until chilled.

To make the marshmallow fluff: Put the aquafaba into the bowl of a stand mixer fitted with the whisk attachment and beat the liquid on medium speed until foamy. Raise the speed to high and beat until the mixture has expanded considerably and forms peaks, about 15 to 20 minutes.

   With the mixer running, add the superfine sugar 2 tablespoons (30 g) at a time and then add the vanilla powder. The fluff should form soft peaks.

To assemble: Divide the pudding among 4 small bowls and then place about ⅓ cup (32 g) of marshmallow fluff into each bowl. Using a kitchen torch, toast the top of the fluff lightly. (If you do not have a torch, you can omit this step.) Top the dessert with the crushed graham crackers and chocolate chips. Serve immediately.

YIELD: **4 servings**

FOR THE CHOCOLATE PUDDING:

1½ cups (345 g) mashed avocado

½ cup (40 g) unsweetened cocoa powder

⅓ cup (59 g) Medjool dates, pitted and soaked in warm water for 15 minutes

1 to 2 tablespoons (15 to 28 ml) date soaking water

3 tablespoons (45 ml) maple syrup

¼ teaspoon salt

FOR THE MARSHMALLOW FLUFF:

⅓ cup (80 ml) aquafaba (the liquid drained from a can of chickpeas—see note on page 114)

½ cup (120 g) organic superfine cane sugar

½ teaspoon vanilla powder

FOR THE ASSEMBLY:

¼ cup (21 g) vegan graham crackers, crushed

¼ cup (44 g) soy-free, nut-free vegan mini chocolate chips

- If you can't find organic superfine sugar, whir regular organic cane sugar in a food processor.

- There will be a lot of marshmallow fluff left over from this recipe—use it in the Cookies 'n' Cream Dip (page 189) or the Kiwi Pistachio Mousse with Praline Crumbles (page 184)!

- Vegan graham crackers can be tricky to find, but I've had luck when checking the ingredient labels on kids' graham crackers.

KIWI PISTACHIO MOUSSE WITH PRALINE CRUMBLES

GLUTEN-FREE • SOY-FREE

Icy cool yet fluffy, the kiwi-pistachio mousse pairs perfectly with crunchy praline crumbles in this stunning dessert. Juicy kiwi pieces and crushed pistachios top it off.

To make the kiwi pistachio mousse: Put the aquafaba in the bowl of a stand mixer fitted with the whisk attachment and beat the liquid on medium speed until foamy. Raise the speed to high and beat until the mixture has expanded considerably and forms peaks, about 15 to 20 minutes.

While the aquafaba is whipping, purée the kiwi and pistachios together in a blender. You may need to scrape the sides down a couple of times to get everything. When the aquafaba is forming peaks, slowly add the powdered sugar to the mixer, along with the cream of tartar.

Once all is combined and fluffy, carefully fold the kiwi pistachio mixture in with the aquafaba until combined; you must be gentle or it will deflate and turn into a weird pudding. Divide the mixture among 4 small bowls and freeze them for 1 to 2 hours.

To make the praline crumbles: Place all of the praline ingredients in a saucepan and heat, covered, over medium heat. Get a baking sheet ready by lining it with parchment paper or a silicone baking mat.

Bring the mixture to a boil, stirring often and making sure none of the sugar crystals are missed. Cook until all of the sugar has dissolved and then test the texture by dropping a tiny amount into a glass of cold water. When picked out, it should be soft and flexible.

FOR THE KIWI PISTACHIO MOUSSE:

½ cup (120 ml) aquafaba (the liquid drained from a can of chickpeas—see note on page 114)

3 kiwis, peeled and chopped

½ cup (62 g) raw pistachios

½ cup (60 g) organic powdered sugar

⅛ teaspoon cream of tartar

FOR THE PRALINE CRUMBLES:

½ cup (62 g) chopped roasted pistachios

¼ cup (48 g) organic brown sugar

¼ cup (48 g) organic cane sugar

2 tablespoons (28 ml) unsweetened soy-free nondairy milk

2 tablespoons (28 g) coconut oil

1 teaspoon vanilla extract

Pinch of salt

FOR THE ASSEMBLY:

2 tablespoons (15 g) crushed roasted pistachios

1 kiwi, peeled and diced

Take the pan off the stove and stir vigorously until the praline pulls away from the sides of the pan and loses its gloss, becoming more matte. Place 4 spoonfuls onto the baking sheet and let cool for 10 minutes.

To assemble: Once the kiwi pistachio mousse is frozen, break apart 1 praline over each bowl and then top with crushed pistachios and kiwi. Serve immediately.

YIELD: 4 servings

SNAPPY GINGER CREAM CHEESE FROSTING TRIFLE

I have always seen trifles as layer cakes that you don't have to worry about frosting perfectly, but that are still gorgeous in their own right and definitely delicious. This spiced ginger cake trifle is perfect for a holiday gathering, with its decadent cream cheese frosting and crunchy gingersnaps. Plus, you can make it a day ahead.

(continued on next page)

(continued from previous page)

To make the ginger cake: Preheat the oven to 350°F (180°C, or gas mark 4) and lightly grease an 8 inch (20 cm)-square baking pan.

In a large bowl, sift together the all-purpose flour, pastry flour, sugar, baking soda, cinnamon, ginger, nutmeg, salt, and cloves. In a small bowl, whisk together the cold water, olive oil, white vinegar, molasses, and vanilla.

Add the wet mixture to the dry mixture and whisk together until smooth. Transfer the batter to the baking dish and bake for 35 to 40 minutes until a toothpick inserted in the center comes out clean. Place the pan on a cooling rack for 1 hour.

To make the cream cheese frosting: In a medium bowl, cream the vegan cream cheese and vegan butter together with a handheld electric mixer on high speed. Adjust the speed to medium-high and add the powdered sugar, ½ cup (60 g) at a time. Whip until smooth and then add the vanilla and salt, whipping until combined. Refrigerate for 30 minutes before layering.

To assemble: Break half of the cake into smaller pieces and place in the bottom of a large glass (preferably clear) bowl. Carefully spread half of the frosting over it and sprinkle half of the crushed gingersnaps over the frosting. Repeat the layers and serve. This can be made 1 day ahead and stored in the refrigerator until ready to serve.

YIELD: 6 to 8 servings

> Serving this dessert family-style is easy, but if you want to up the fancy factor, assemble and present this in 6 small sundae bowls as single servings.

FOR THE GINGER CAKE:

1 cup (125 g) unbleached all-purpose flour

½ cup (60 g) whole wheat pastry flour

1 cup (192 g) organic cane sugar

1 teaspoon baking soda

1 teaspoon ground cinnamon

1 teaspoon ground ginger

¼ teaspoon ground nutmeg

¼ teaspoon salt

Pinch of ground cloves

¾ cup (180 ml) cold water

¼ cup (60 ml) olive oil

1 tablespoon (15 ml) white vinegar

1 tablespoon (20 g) molasses

1 teaspoon vanilla extract

FOR THE CREAM CHEESE FROSTING:

8 ounces (225 g) vegan cream cheese

¼ cup (56 g) vegan butter

2 cups (240 g) organic powdered sugar

2 teaspoons vanilla extract

Pinch of salt

FOR THE ASSEMBLY:

1 cup (21 g) crushed vegan gingersnaps

COOKIES 'N' CREAM DIP

SOY-FREE • NUT-FREE

Don't let savory dips and spreads have all the fun at your next party. Surprise people with this fluffy, sweet dip, and once the bowl is licked clean, shock the pants off them when you say that it is made with bean water!

To make the cookies: In a small bowl, stir together the flaxseed with the water and let set for 5 minutes. Using a stand or handheld electric mixer, whip the sugar and coconut oil on high speed until combined. Still mixing, add the flaxseed mixture and nondairy milk; beat until fluffy.

Sift the flour, cocoa powder, baking powder, and salt into a bowl. Add the dry mixture to the wet mixture and blend on medium speed until the cookie dough is crumbly but sticks together when pressed or squeezed. Form into a dough ball and refrigerate for 10 minutes.

Preheat the oven to 350°F (180°C, or gas mark 4) and line a large baking sheet with a silicone baking mat or parchment paper.

Lightly flour your workspace and rolling pin and roll out the cookie dough to ⅛ inch (3 mm) thick. Using a 2 inch (5 cm)-round cookie cutter, cut out the cookies and place on the baking sheet, repeating process with remaining dough.

Bake the cookies for 9 to 10 minutes or until firm. Transfer the cookies to a cooling rack. They will further harden as they cool.

To make the dip: Put the aquafaba in the bowl of a stand mixer fitted with the whisk attachment and beat the liquid on medium speed until foamy. Raise the speed to high and beat until the mixture has expanded considerably and peaks, about 15 to 20 minutes.

Slowly add the powdered sugar while the mixer is running as well as the cream of tartar and vanilla powder. Place half of the cookies in a food processor and pulse until crumbly. Carefully fold the cookies into the aquafaba fluff until combined and then transfer to a bowl and serve with the remaining cookies and apple slices for dipping. You can also store this dip in your refrigerator until ready to serve.

YIELD: 4 servings

FOR THE COOKIES:

1½ teaspoons ground flaxseed

1 tablespoon (15 ml) hot water

¼ cup (48 g) plus 2 teaspoons organic cane sugar

¼ cup (56 g) coconut oil, at room temperature

1½ teaspoons unsweetened soy-free, nut-free nondairy milk

⅔ cup (83 g) unbleached all-purpose flour

⅓ cup (27 g) unsweetened cocoa powder

¼ teaspoon baking powder

Pinch of salt

FOR THE DIP:

⅓ cup (80 ml) aquafaba (the liquid drained from a can of chickpeas—see note on page 114)

1 cup (120 g) organic powdered sugar

¼ teaspoon cream of tartar

¼ teaspoon vanilla powder

Apple slices, for serving (optional)

Chapter 7

BOWL ESSENTIALS

SAUCES, SPREADS, DIPS, AND DRIZZLES

You cannot have a bowl cookbook without a section of satisfying sauces, savory spreads, dependable dips, and divine drizzles! Plus, there are a couple of other tasty, multipurpose recipes included here that you can use on your bowl journey.

IRRESISTIBLE RANCH DRESSING

GLUTEN-FREE • SOY-FREE

Out of all of the recipes on my blog that get the best reviews, this ranch recipe is a clear winner! It has the perfect balance of creaminess, seasoning, and tang, and it pretty much goes with everything.

Drain and rinse the cashews and place them in a blender along with the remaining ingredients. Blend until completely smooth. Add more water if the dressing is too thick since it will continue to thicken in the refrigerator.

Transfer to an airtight container and store in the refrigerator for up to 2 weeks.

YIELD: About 1¾ cups (420 g)

1 cup (140 g) raw cashews, soaked in warm water for 30 minutes

⅔ cup (160 ml) unsweetened soy-free nondairy milk

¼ cup (60 ml) water

2 tablespoons (28 ml) white vinegar

1 tablespoon (15 ml) lemon juice

1¾ teaspoons onion powder

1¼ teaspoons salt, or to taste

1 teaspoon garlic powder

1 teaspoon dried parsley

¼ teaspoon agave nectar

¼ teaspoon freshly ground black pepper

⅛ teaspoon dried dill

STRAWBERRY BARBECUE SAUCE

GLUTEN-FREE OPTION • NUT-FREE

Making your own barbecue sauce can be such a fun experience in that it is much easier than you might expect. Changing the standard base of tomatoes to strawberries adds a different tartness to this tangy sauce.

Place all of the ingredients in a blender and purée until completely smooth. Transfer the sauce to a saucepan over medium heat and cook until it begins to simmer. Lower the heat and stir occasionally until the sauce has thickened enough to coat the back of a spoon, about 7 to 10 minutes.

Transfer to an airtight container and store in the refrigerator for up to 2 weeks.

YIELD: 1½ cups (375 g)

2 cups (340 g) chopped fresh strawberries

2 tablespoons (28 ml) white vinegar

2 tablespoons (28 ml) maple syrup

4 teaspoons (20 ml) vegan Worcestershire sauce (gluten-free, if necessary)

4 teaspoons (27 g) unsulfured molasses

2 teaspoons yellow mustard

1 teaspoon liquid aminos or tamari

1 teaspoon liquid smoke (gluten-free, if necessary)

1 teaspoon onion powder

1 teaspoon garlic powder

½ teaspoon chili powder

½ teaspoon paprika

⅓ teaspoon cayenne pepper

¼ teaspoon ground turmeric

Salt and freshly ground black pepper, to taste

CHEEZY CHEDDAR SAUCE

GLUTEN-FREE • SOY-FREE • SUGAR-FREE

Ultra-creamy and so very versatile, this cheezy cheddar sauce can be used in a multitude of ways. In this book alone you'll find it in the Biscuit Nacho Bowl (page 33), Buffalo Jackfruit Dip (page 47), Buffalo Chickpea Mac 'n' Cheeze (page 116), and Snack Shack Chili Billy (page 126)!

1 cup (140 g) raw cashews, soaked in warm water for 30 minutes

1 cup (225 ml) water

¼ cup (15 g) nutritional yeast

1 tablespoon (8 g) tapioca starch

1 tablespoon (16 g) tomato paste

1 tablespoon (15 ml) coconut vinegar or apple cider vinegar

2 teaspoons onion powder

1½ teaspoons Dijon mustard

1 teaspoon sea salt

Pinch of ground turmeric

Drain and rinse the cashews and place them in a blender along with the remaining ingredients. Blend until completely smooth, adding more water if the sauce seems too thick. Transfer to a saucepan over medium-low heat, bringing it to a low simmer and stirring frequently to prevent clumping. Once the starch has broken down and the sauce has thickened slightly, about 3 to 5 minutes, remove from the heat.

Transfer to an airtight container and store in the refrigerator for up to 2 weeks (that's more of a dare because there is no way it's lasting that long).

YIELD: 2 cups (430 g)

SILKY SOUR CREAM

GLUTEN-FREE • NUT-FREE • SUGAR-FREE

Here's a simple, protein-rich sour cream to dollop on all sorts of things!

1 package (12 ounces or 340 g) firm silken tofu

1½ tablespoons (20 ml) apple cider vinegar

1 tablespoon (15 ml) olive or vegetable oil

⅛ teaspoon sea salt

Place all of the ingredients in a food processor and purée until very smooth. Transfer to an airtight container and store in the refrigerator for up to 2 weeks.

YIELD: 1 generous cup (230 g or more)

QUICKY MARINARA SAUCE

GLUTEN-FREE • SOY-FREE • NUT-FREE • SUGAR-FREE

Marinara is one of my favorite dipping sauces, probably because I love tomato foods a little too much. Make this fast and tasty sauce in a whopping 5 minutes!

Place all of the ingredients in a small saucepan and bring to a simmer over medium heat. Cook for 5 minutes or until hot and thickened slightly.

Use immediately or transfer to an airtight container and store in the refrigerator for up to 2 weeks.

YIELD: 1½ cups (368 g)

1 can (14.5 ounces, or 410 g) tomato sauce

½ teaspoon dried Italian seasoning

½ teaspoon onion powder

¼ teaspoon garlic powder

Pinch of crushed red pepper flakes

Salt, to taste

> If your marinara is too acidic for your tastes, stir in ½ teaspoon organic cane sugar along with the herbs and spices.

BASIC SEITAN

NUT-FREE • SUGAR-FREE

Making seitan from scratch is the only way to really enjoy eating it; plus it is economical and surprisingly easy to make. This basic seitan recipe can be easily customized through changes in seasoning to suit your own tastes. And the recipes you use it in will further customize the seitan, through grilling, roasting, or other cooking techniques.

½ cup (50 g) vital wheat gluten

¼ teaspoon garlic powder

¼ teaspoon onion powder

¼ teaspoon salt-free poultry seasoning

⅛ teaspoon ground ginger

1½ cups (355 ml) vegetable broth, heated, divided

1 tablespoon (15 ml) liquid aminos

In a large bowl, whisk together the vital wheat gluten, garlic powder, onion powder, poultry seasoning, and ground ginger. Add ½ cup (120 ml) of the warm vegetable broth and the liquid aminos to the dry mixture, stir to combine, and then knead for 2 minutes.

Cut the seitan into 12 nugget-size pieces. Warm the remaining 1 cup (235 ml) vegetable broth in a saucepan over medium-low heat. Add the seitan and partially cover with a lid. Simmer for 20 minutes, flipping the pieces halfway through and stirring occasionally so that they don't stick together.

Place the seitan on paper towels to drain and cool. Use according to the recipe of your choice. Store in an airtight container in the refrigerator for up to 5 days.

YIELD: 4 servings

TEMPTING TEMPEH BACON

GLUTEN-FREE • NUT-FREE

Smoky, sweet, salty, and slightly crunchy, what more could you want from a vegan bacon?

Whisk together the water, liquid aminos, maple syrup, liquid smoke, onion powder, smoked paprika, and black pepper in a shallow dish with a lid. Cut the tempeh into ¼ inch (6 mm)-wide strips and place them in the dish to marinate for at least 4 hours.

Melt the coconut oil in a sauté pan over medium heat. Add the tempeh strips to the pan, along with 2 tablespoons (28 ml) of the marinade. Cook until the liquid has evaporated and the tempeh browns. Flip the pieces over to brown them on the other side. Repeat with the remaining tempeh. Serve warm. Store in an airtight container in the refrigerator for up to 5 days.

YIELD: 4 servings

¼ cup (60 ml) water

3 tablespoons (45 ml) liquid aminos

2 tablespoons (30 ml) maple syrup

1 tablespoon (15 ml) gluten-free liquid smoke

½ teaspoon onion powder

½ teaspoon smoked paprika

Pinch of freshly ground black pepper

1 package (8 ounces, or 225 g) tempeh

1 tablespoon (14 g) coconut oil

SIMPLE GUACAMOLE

GLUTEN-FREE • SOY-FREE • NUT-FREE • SUGAR-FREE

Guacamole is a food group, right? Oh, it's not? Well, it should be. Here is my no-frills guacamole recipe to fill all of your mashed avocado needs.

1 cup (230 g) mashed avocado

2 tablespoons (20 g) diced white onion

1 tablespoon (1 g) minced fresh cilantro

1 tablespoon (15 ml) lime juice

⅛ teaspoon sea salt

Place all of the ingredients in a bowl and mash together with a fork until combined. Chill for 20 minutes before serving.

YIELD: 2 servings

SMOKY TAHINI SAUCE

GLUTEN-FREE • NUT-FREE • SUGAR-FREE

Tahini is made from sesame seeds, which are not only high in iron, but also full of flavor and even a little bitter (in a good way). Combine that with smoky spices and you have a delectable, savory sauce for topping bowls of all kinds.

In a small bowl, whisk all of the ingredients together until smooth. Add more water for a thinner sauce, if desired. Serve immediately or store in an airtight container in the refrigerator for up to 10 days.

YIELD: ¾ cup (180 g)

- 5 tablespoons (75 g) tahini
- ¼ cup (60 ml) water
- 1 tablespoon (4 g) nutritional yeast
- 1 tablespoon (15 ml) apple cider vinegar
- 2 teaspoons liquid aminos or tamari
- 2 teaspoons gluten-free liquid smoke
- ¾ teaspoon onion powder
- ½ teaspoon smoked paprika
- ¼ teaspoon ground cumin
- Pinch of cayenne pepper
- Salt, to taste

CHOCOLATE SAUCE

GLUTEN-FREE • SOY-FREE • NUT-FREE

This sweetly simple chocolate sauce also doubles as a chocolate shell; it will harden when placed in the refrigerator or freezer or on top of frozen desserts. Now everything can be coated in chocolate!

Whisk all of the ingredients together until smooth. Serve immediately or store in an airtight container in the refrigerator for up to 1 month. Heat in the microwave for 30 to 45 seconds to melt.

YIELD: About ½ cup (150 g)

- 2½ tablespoons (40 ml) maple syrup or agave nectar
- 2 tablespoons (28 g) coconut oil, melted
- 2½ tablespoons (13 g) unsweetened cocoa powder

DATE CARAMEL

GLUTEN-FREE • SOY-FREE

I am not a huge fan of when people compare fruits to candy—because let's be real, they are not the same. In the case of dates, though, they may just be right. Whip up this healthy alternative to caramel and drizzle it on your favorite sweet treats.

In a bowl or cup, cover the dates with the warm water and soak them for 15 minutes so that they soften. Place the dates, the date soaking water, coconut sugar, lemon juice, and salt in a blender and purée until completely smooth. This may take scraping the sides of the blender down a couple of times.

If you would like a hot caramel, transfer the sauce to a saucepan and warm it over medium-low heat for 5 minutes, stirring occasionally. Serve. Store in an airtight container in the refrigerator for up to 1 week.

YIELD: 1 cup (225 g)

8 Medjool dates (192 g), pitted

½ cup plus 2 tablespoons (150 ml) warm water

1 tablespoon (9 g) coconut sugar

1½ teaspoons lemon juice

⅛ teaspoon salt

SWEET CASHEW CREAM

GLUTEN-FREE • SOY-FREE

When I first made this ambrosial creamy sauce, I had my mother test it out on a dessert. Let me tell you, I'm glad that I was supervising this task or else she would have eaten the entire container with a spoon. Yes, it is that good.

Drain and rinse the cashews and then add them to a blender, along with the water, maple syrup, vanilla bean seeds, and salt. Blend until completely smooth, adding more water if necessary to adjust the thickness. Serve immediately or store in an airtight container in the refrigerator for up to 1 week.

YIELD: 1 cup (230 g)

1 cup (140 g) raw cashews, soaked in warm water for 30 minutes

½ cup (120 ml) water

3 tablespoons (45 ml) maple syrup

Seeds scraped from ½ of a vanilla bean

Pinch of salt

ACKNOWLEDGMENTS

There is no shortage of people in my life who I want to thank, who have helped me in one way or another throughout my journey as a food blogger, photographer, and now, cookbook author. I could go on forever, and if you know me, you know that I am not exaggerating, but I would like to single out a few people and say how fortunate I am to have them as friends and family.

First, there is no way I could have even dreamed of doing what I do if it weren't for my parents, Ralph and Marilyn Sobon. You two have supported me in so many ways, whether it be helping with school, housing me when I changed career paths from designer to professional food-player-wither, and helping wash mountains of dishes after cranking out many recipes for deadlines. You are also my most valued quality assurance personnel because you are always up front with me, and you are not vegan! Thank you so much for all that you have done. I know that I cannot come close to repaying you for it.

Next, I'd like to thank my sisters, Katie and Stacie, for their continued support and for believing in me, as well as for being compassionate to others and especially their companion animals.

To Corey, I sincerely thank you for listening, providing emotional support, and occasionally joining my parents for QA testing.

What is life without friends? Boring, I tell you! This is where the thanking gets tough because I really could rattle on for hours and hours. But I will start by thanking my mentors and friends, Joni Marie Newman and JL Fields, for all of their useful input, answering of my questions, and being there when work got tough and I needed help in more ways than one. Erin Wysocarski and Michelle Davis, thank you for your help in assisting me for a few days on this book; it was essential to its creation and I cannot thank you enough!

To my friends Caroline, Kelly, Tim, Megan, and Tristan, thank you for helping me clear out my fridge when food overflowed from it like Niagara Falls, for this book, and for many of the other projects I have worked on. More important, thank you for being there for so many different occasions throughout our time together. I feel lucky to call you my friends!

And last but not least, a huge thank-you to all of my recipe testers: Ted Lai, Jenny Bradley, Sarah de la Cruz, Nicole Keene, Brianne Hazekamp, Lacy Davis, Jackie Chapman, Lauren Kaufman, Don Gaines, Leslie Conn, Jennifer Gallagher, Helen Pitlick, Jeffery Eggleston, Jared Bigman, Amy Katz, Billie Fasulo, Rachel Johnson, Shelley Osborne, Katya Galbis, and Kelly McKenzie. You are all so invaluable and truly a key component to the success of this awesome bowl cookbook—you totally kicked ass!

ABOUT THE AuTHoR

Jackie Sobon is a food photographer, recipe developer, and author specializing in vegan food. She is the founder of the popular food blog *Vegan Yack Attack*, which has been showcasing her creative recipes and stunning photography since 2011 and has been placed on many top blog lists. Her work has been featured on websites such as KTLA News, ABC News (Good Morning America), *VegNews*, Kris Carr, PureWow, Babble, and BuzzFeed. Jackie has photographed cookbooks for the likes of Jason Wrobel, Happy Herbivore, and other plant-based authors. She has self-published three e-books, contributed to *We Love Quinoa* (Taunton Press), and is the Sweet Treats columnist for *VegNews* magazine.

INDEX